T0096646

I Wanted to Say . . .
I LOVE YOU

Isalou Regen & Sabchu Rinpoche

I Wanted to Say . . .
I LOVE YOU

Isalou Regen & Sabchu Rinpoche

Translated from the French by Jourdie Ross

RABSEL
PUBLICATIONS

ORIGINAL TITLE:
Je voulais te dire ... I Love You
©Rabsel Éditions 2018

The translator thanks Arnaud Duhayon, Audrey Dessérières, Louise Munoz,
and Marge Erickson.

RABSEL PUBLICATIONS
16, rue de Babylone
76430 La Remuée, France
www.rabsel.com
contact@rabsel.com

This project was supported by the DRAC and Normandy Region under the FADEL
Normandie, France.

© Rabsel Publications, La Remuée, France, 2019
ISBN 978-2-36017-009-8

Contents

Preface

I Love You

Three words as universal as a score of music; three words understood around the world; three words that mark a change in one's life or in a relationship, yet three words that time can also fade.

This book tells a story of self-rediscovery following a romantic breakup.

The path begins with the unplanned meeting of a great Tibetan master. Thanks to this encounter, it is rich with interviews, wisdom, and humanity.

This tale is also a journey—from Normandy in France to Bodh Gaya, India, passing through Paris, Toronto, and, finally, the mountains of Tibet.

We follow Isalou from an idea of romantic love—one that is eternal and a bit obsessive—on her odyssey to discover another kind of love: one focused on others rather than oneself and called compassion.

This compassion has become so rare today that for some, and, for too many of our leaders, it no longer exists. This compassion is a strange paradox in our early 21st century, where the retreat into selfishness, fear, and hatred is spreading with epidemic speed.

Compassion, even greater than a remedy, is a force that can change the world.

So please, take full advantage of your reading!

May your life be beautiful.

Marc Levy

Introduction

How many thousands of people say "I love you" every day? Is it possible that these three little ordinary words could contain all the truth and challenge of love?

He and I, we called each other *Love, My Wonder,* and *My Prince.*

Excuse the cliché, but the only witnesses to our first "I love you" were the moon and Saint-Eustace Cathedral. It made the moment perfect. Angels' breath was blowing on both of our hearts. Only the bells reminded us of our human condition . . . our showing of *Dallas Buyers Club* was starting, and we were late. Our *us* suddenly came to life in the perfect fit of our two hands. Starting from this moment, I became the heroine in a fairytale; I only had eyes for my prince, and my prince only had eyes for me. He crossed all of Paris between two business meetings just to place a kiss on my lips. My everyday blossomed with his touch; he made my morning cup of tea and handed it to me with whispered sweet nothings. He sent me text messages bursting with red hearts or *I love you I love you I love you I love you I love you x 100*. In my phone, he was the letter A, for *Amour*. *Amour* was first, at the very top of my contact list. No one before him. Everything for him. We shared our happiness on Facebook, but we remained the sole inhabitants of our little world. Hand in hand, on sidewalks, in dark rooms . . . our fingers laced together on the tablecloths of Paris. Tied to the strength of his hands and his love, I no longer feared anything. On my wedding dress, I had a declaration of love inspired by Eva Peron embroidered like a great tattoo, "He is a condor who flies high . . . I love to fly with him and contemplate the wonderful vastness." Every evening, we fell asleep melting into one another with this pressing—and childish—question, which became our bedtime ritual, "Big spoon or little spoon?" We even fell asleep, at times, lips locked with lips in an unending kiss, one we wished would be eternal. "We are one," he often wrote to me . . .

I had never lived anything like this.

Sometime later, I found myself in a movie theater with my friend Liz, watching the latest version of *Beauty and the Beast*. My heart in tatters, torn into a thousand pieces.

"Love, we need to stop this . . ." he had said to me, the Sunday night before. After a year-and-a-half of marriage and three years of cloudless happiness—at least from my perspective, he said he no longer felt happy; he had hit bottom, couldn't even work out the how or why and didn't know how to "reach the surface without starting fresh." The words were like an axe to my heart. Then he left me.

I'll never shake away the pain
I close my eyes but she's still there
Now I know she'll never leave me
Even as she runs away
She will still torment me
Calm me, hurt me[1]

Once Upon a Time . . .

The story of this book begins with these words from "Evermore", sung by the Beast on the ramparts of his castle, distraught and hopeless after Belle's departure to save her father.

Wasting in my lonely tower
I'll think of all that might have been
Waiting here for evermore

Stop! I had quite enough hopelessness of my own already. And I had also had enough of absorbing these doses of *I will wait, forever, for always* based on this culture of romantic love woven from one thread of attachment and the next of heartache. First prize goes to the fairytales of our childhood that always end well with the famous *happily ever after*.

Why fill our imaginations with fantasies if, later on, real life looks nothing like them? As for the long, tranquil stream to come; get out the oars . . .

Of course, we wind up feeling helpless in the face of complicated love affairs that leave behind sensations of

---

1 Translator's Note: Dan Stevens, "Evermore," by Alan Menken and Tim Rice, in *Beauty and the Beast*: Original Motion Picture Soundtrack, Walt Disney Records, 2017, MP3.

failure, shame, guilt, and low self-esteem. Even if we know how to deal with heartbreak, we always secretly hope, in our heart of hearts, that we'll find Love with a capital L that will last our whole lives. These ideas of eternal love between a man and a woman—he's hers and she's his—are tough to get over. They are so tightly wound into our concepts that they make us forget that they are no more than cultural constructs.

LOVE: noun, intense feeling of affection or sexual attraction for a person

Humans have not experienced love in the same way since the beginning of time, and love itself does not necessarily match up with our current beliefs. We have intelligently adjusted our concepts according to society's needs and challenges: collaborative love for survival and the reproduction of our species; political love to unite territories and preserve titles. Courtly love (idealistic), platonic love (chaste), the love of a woman for several men (polyandry), the love of a man for several women (polygamy), monogamous and faithful Christian love, romantic love (passionate) . . . All of these concepts are only relative and definitely fluctuate.

Today, the vision of romantic love born from the Christian ideal and based on monogamy dominates our way of thinking. It's a very nice model, but one which seems to be breaking down, considering the decline in the number of marriages, the increase in divorce, the spread of celibacy, the success of extra-marital meetup sites, and the appearance of new ideas like polyamory[2] or sologamy.[3]

On a certain level, the passionate idea of melting into one another, the *we are one*, faithful for life, functions less well in the modern day. Between the aspiration for personal realization and the fantasy of romantic love, there's a blockage . . . this is even more true in the time of feminine emancipation. And it remains true even in the face of life's various disturbances like hormonal needs, the desire for another person, the thirst for newness, boredom, and melancholy.

So, the big question: What is love beyond these cultural fluctuations and preconceived models?

What is really at work when, pupils dilated and eyes bright with hope, we exchange this declaration, "I love you"? Why is this love that gives us wings and anchors our faith in ourselves and another—that lets us go beyond ourselves—so difficult to keep alive day after day and even more difficult to make last in the long term? Is there an inevitable expiration date, like a jar of strawberry jam? Does it really only last three years? What catches up with us and makes everything complicated?

Where is the glitch? What is the road to salvation?

Fortunately, even when we have hit rock bottom, there is life and its invitations. After the showing of *Beauty and the Beast*, I got a message from my friend Nicolas that opened up a door. "There are some teachings this weekend in Normandy on love and attachment. That would be good for you, right? You coming?"

---

2   Polyamory: A new ethic of love relationships in which partners consider each other capable of loving several people at the same time without culpability.

3   Sologamy: A new trend involving marriage to oneself, with the goal of enjoying one's own company without waiting to be fulfilled by another.

Wasting in my lonely tower
I'll think of all that might have been
Waiting here for evermore

Good timing indeed! I was in serious need of relief and some clarity on the subject, as I could not understand what was happening to me. And furthermore, the teachings would be given by Sabchu Rinpoche, a Tibetan Buddhist master passing through France. *Master:* that means lots of wisdom, a ton of study, profound understanding of the mind's functioning, a wide-open heart, and an immense reservoir of love and compassion. Compassion—I found this word vague, overused, far-removed from our ordinary lives, and, in the end, reserved for monks. But I'll admit I was in great need of it. I had so much misunderstanding and pain inside me.

The very first time that I felt what a master could be was while watching Scorsese's *Kundun,* a portrait of the Dalai Lama. The film really got to me. To the point that the final sentences of dialogue were like an arrow straight to my heart, filling my eyes with tears.

The film's final dialogue: After having crossed Tibet with much difficulty on horseback and by buffalo to seek refuge in India, the staggering, exhausted Dalai Lama finally arrives at the border. A stalwart customs officer comes to meet him, greets him, and asks him,

"With all respect sir, may I ask, 'Who are you?'"

"What you see before you is a man, a simple monk."

"Are you the Lord Buddha?"

"I think I am a reflection, like the moon on water. When you see me, when I try to be a good man, you see yourself."

replies the Dalai lama with infinite tenderness.

With these words, the film continues with images of a sand mandala being swept away as Tibetan horns play in the background. It is like a bolt of lightning. There, you understand that what you can see in this man is nothing other than yourself. The majesty, the strength of compassion, and the courage that you see in him are your own as well. He is only a reflection. A reflection who knew how to brush away the dust of his ego to let us see ourselves in the utmost beauty. Waves of inner shock and revelation. It is reassuring to know that beings exist whose sole priority is to become better people for the benefit of others. Day after day, teaching after teaching, meditation after meditation, practice after practice, they work on themselves and transform their way of being and thinking in order to become generators of universal love.

Without hesitating for a second, I hopped on the first train at Saint-Lazare Station and left for Normandy. It was a question of survival.

From my first moment in Sabchu Rinpoche's presence, I felt a gentle and profound joy that felt like *home* in my very core. I immediately felt safe. I could finally unload my burden of tears and sadness—eyes swollen, nose running—and dare to be me, to open my heart while feeling completely welcome, heard, understood, loved—at peace, somehow.

The venerable 5th Dilyag Sabchu Rinpoche is a disconcerting Tibetan Buddhist teacher. He is part of this new generation of masters; young—thirty-four years old—super hip and modern, but with a benevolent presence, the disarming smile to go with it, a wise and authentic strength combined with gentle humility and, the cherry on top, an irresistible sense of humor!

Like the Dalai Lama, Sabchu Rinpoche received the traditional Buddhist education and training as well as the rigorous spiritual instruction given to reincarnations of important masters.[4] In addition, Sabchu Rinpoche has a unique asset: he rounded out his Tibetan education with a Western Bachelor's degree in film studies in Canada. Why film? Because "it is a world of images and representations that is so true to our own functioning."

At once a great scholar and a teacher, incredibly skilled at simplifying complex philosophical concepts, Sabchu Rinpoche splits his time between travelling the world to give Dharma[5] teachings, being in meditation retreat, supervising his Karma Kagyü monastery in Swayambhu, Nepal, and writing stories and teachings.

His gentle presence, his vivid teachings on love and compassion—as crystal clear as a mountain lake—did me a world of good. My throat, which had so long been tight with sobs, relaxed, my breathing calmed, my mascara finally stayed on for more than an hour, and, little by little, I began to smile again. Just a few moments beyond my suffering allowed me to reconnect with this immense capacity for love inside of me—this sun, this luminous thing in each of us that the teachings speak about and that could shine like a thousand flames if it was not permanently covered by fog and clouds.

---

4   Translator's Note: This training is specific to each individual lineage of Tibetan Buddhism. Sabchu Rinpoche received the training appropriate for and specific to the Karma Kagyü lineage.

5   The Buddha's teachings.

How could I make this feeling of well-being that arose from the glow of Sabchu Rinpoche's compassion last for more than the few hours I spent with him? How could I connect this luminous, spacious, loving *thing* that eased my heart with my everyday life? Concretely, what do we have to understand about love, and how do we go about being happy from day to day in our romantic relationships, our *romances,* as we're wont to call them?

Being close to this elevated master from the roof of the world, at once modern and erudite, woke my taste for adventure. What if I wrote a book on the subject with Rinpoche?

Only listening to my wish to learn and my sense of spontaneity, I shared my wish with him, and he listened with great interest. I sketched out a plan that he took the time to read. After a bit of consideration, he suggested that we meet the next day to discuss it.

Sabchu Rinpoche began our interview by sharing a personal reflection with me, "I am wondering how a monk with celibacy vows could be a legitimate source on the question of romantic relationships. I have thought quite a bit about it, and I think my contribution could be beneficial for readers of this book. There exists a preconceived notion that a monk can talk about meditation, which is considered his realm of knowledge as opposed to romantic relationships.

I would say that you do not have to get in a boat and sail around the world to understand that the earth is round. Likewise, you do not have to swallow poison to understand what it is. Of course, I am not comparing love to poison. I am talking about understanding. We do not have to experience everything, but we have to understand it correctly."

After this preliminary reflection, he said yes to the book, on one condition: that he could ask me questions about my own story in order to get to know me better and, through me, be able to reach any person who shares this experience, which is, in many ways, universal. Indeed, how many of us on this planet are suffering from heartbreak or lack of love?

The starting shot fired, we pulled out our calendars. We made an appointment to meet in Bodh Gaya, a small city in East India, situated between Kathmandu and Calcutta. What sets this place apart? It is here that the Prince Siddhartha achieved enlightenment beneath the Bodhi tree, thus becoming the Gautama Shakyamuni Buddha with his legendary smile that we all know. Each year, practitioners from around the world come together here to recite aspiration prayers and wishes.

"It is organic," rejoiced Sabchu Rinpoche at the ease with which we managed to sync our schedules. On the train back to Paris, while contemplating a magnificent rainbow in the Normandy sky, I thought to myself, "It's so great when things are easy."

The first thing I did upon arriving home was to put away my boxes of tissues and book a flight to India.

Starting Here, Everything Changed

Written in Bodh Gaya, Paris, Toronto, and the majestic mountains of Tibet, *I Wanted to Say . . . I Love You* is an invitation to understand and experience our romantic relationships through the lens of two-thousand-year-old wisdom.

I wished to explore love by putting three words under a microscope: I LOVE YOU—this famous declaration understood by every inhabitant of our planet. And to do so while being faithful to the Buddhist practice of analysis and understanding based on methodic observation of what is—similar in this way to the scientific method.

"Why English words?" you might ask. [6] For three reasons. First, all the interviews with Sabchu Rinpoche occurred in English. Next, speaking about *I* and not *je* prevents mixing with psychoanalytical or psychological notions . . .[7]

And lastly, I LOVE YOU is like Zidane[8] or Coca Cola—everyone knows them!

I: Who is this *I* that says they love and how does it work?

LOVE: What is this mysterious, multi-faceted emotion that goes on between two people? How can we improve our experience of it?

YOU: Who is this *other* that I say I love, and how do I love them properly?

As for the ending, *happily ever after*, I'll let you see where it takes us.

---

6   Translator's Note: In the original French version, the author used the English words "I love you" rather than the French translations.

7   Translator's Note: For reasons of simplicity and out of respect for the author's further reasons, I have retained the English word "I" despite losing this distinction.

8   Translator's Note: Zinedine Zidane is a French professional soccer coach and former player. He is nationally loved and has been voted best French soccer player of all time in popular polls.

The idea for this structure came to me while thinking of my mother. When I was little, she used to knit Fair Isle sweaters covered in geometric patterns and snowflakes for me. Sometimes the skeins of yarn got tangled, and she would ask me to help her untangle them. I loved the work; it made me think of Ariadne saving Theseus from the minotaur's labyrinth. In the same way, amidst my reflections on love, I had the idea of separating out the skeins and following the central thread of each one.

Sabchu Rinpoche's words, beyond a simple shift in perspective, literally transformed my vision of love and my way of living. It's a joyful and truly freeing revolution. Of course, I would have liked to have learned everything he gave me BEFORE going through with a lightning-fast wedding worthy of a bad romantic comedy, but that's not how it panned out. Doubtless, I needed to go through the heartbreak to write this and to find the path of this inner sun. May my mistakes serve your own happiness!

I would like to share three wishes with you from the bottom of my heart:

The first is to succeed in presenting to you, as faithfully as possible, all that the venerable 5th Dilyag Sabchu Rinpoche had the generosity to transmit to me. Me, just a girl next door who has, in her tiny hands, precious treasures that come from a long and impressive line of great spiritual masters. With all my heart, I wish to be worthy of this challenge and sufficiently capable of not denaturing or transforming anything in an inappropriate way.

My second wish is that this book helps save you time and boxes of tissues.

My third and final wish is that, beyond talking to you

about love, this book gives you love. And tons of it!

Wishing you a happy journey into compassion.

It is organic!

I

**India
#LookInside**

1. Isalou
"Spread out in Pieces, Like a Puzzle."[9]

On December 11, I arrived in Bodh Gaya. Since my child-hood, I had dreamed of going to India—the land of Mahatma Gandhi, Gautama Buddha, and now the very maternal Amma.[10] When I set foot on the ground of this country of contrasts, the place seduced me on contact. An uninterrupted chorus of honking horns, cars, bicycles, motorcycles, rickshaws; wild drivers passing on the left and right; others driving on the side of the road or in the wrong direction; passing crowds of little uniformed schoolchildren here; cows in the middle of the road there; goats, calves, pigs, dogs with their heads in the trash scrounging for something to eat—everything was noisy and chaotic!

---

9   Famous retort from George Lautner's film *Crooks in Clover*.
     Translator's Note: *Crooks in Clover*, DVD, directed by George Lautner (France: Gaumont, 1963).
10   Mata Amritanandamayi, better known by the name Amma ("mother" in Hindi), an Indian saint and guru.

A kind of feverish anarchy in which you feel like you have to assert yourself just to survive. Paradoxically, there was also a certain gentleness and joy floating through it, maybe due to the tenderness I found in the gazes of passersby.

After my arrival at the hotel, I jumped right into my first meeting with Sabchu Rinpoche. There was just enough time for a quick shower, change of clothes, and makeup—the basics after many hours on the plane. Before heading off, I made a quick stop in front of the mirror and gave myself a wide smile. It's a ritual I started after the breakup to help me keep my head above water. Smiling is my antidote to sadness and my humble weapon in the quest to reconquer happiness. It is proven that smiling lowers levels of the stress hormone cortisol in the body and stimulates the production of positive hormones, so I use and abuse as a way of saving my skin.

Since my separation, I had slept badly, my brain resembled the chaos of the Indian streets, and desire was . . . dead! I was hungry for nothing and no one. Cut-off, cold, "spread out in little pieces, like a puzzle." A mess, basically! So, smiling had become vital for me, a real energy that kept me tied to life, to my own will, and to movement. "We have to move forward in life, my dear; we don't have a choice," as my dear mother used to say. With this ritual smile each morning to begin the day, I moved forward. Little by little, I found the strength to take off my wedding ring—a truly wrenching moment—to clear out the past by throwing away old photos and belongings, to grieve, and to take back my last name. It is a real ordeal to find oneself again and to have to change identity. I was no longer Mrs., "wife of." I was single again. Isalou, alone, without the *us*, the *one* that we melted into—a complicity filled with one another.

There is a joke in French, "Pinchmo and Pinchme are on a boat. Pinchmo falls off; who's left?" Sitting there, with my ego out in the cold, I could have asked myself the same thing. Who's left? What is *Isalou*, and who is she, really? Looking in the mirror, I could see that I have a body that is 5'3" and slim, and I knew that the interior is made up of thirty trillion cells, seventy percent water, and some electric currents. I also have a consciousness that allows me to see myself, to think about it, and to define myself: I am a woman, blond, mother, friend, gluten-free vegetarian, author, etc. I feel various sensations: hunger, tiredness, cold, hot . . . and some crazy wild emotions: sadness, anxiety, joy, anger, stress, etc. But all of this still does not answer my fundamental question: who am I?

After several years of analysis, of therapy, of psychotherapy—in group and on my own, various workshops of all kinds, transactional analysis, NLP, *rebirth*, shamanism, etc.—I am very pleased to know my totem animal, my limiting beliefs, and to know that we have three psychic zones: the id, the ego, and superego, but the most comical part of all is that I still do not know who is really flying the plane! Of course, not knowing doesn't prevent me from living each day, but I am still pretty tired of advancing in the dark like a mole, battered by the storms of life.

In light—the fairly weak light—of these observations, I also finally asked myself how I loved. What was really the nature of the love that I felt? Based on what, since that feeling is a big artistic blur? Unknown desires, fantasies, fears, the need for security, the wish to possess or control, some sad, narcissistic neurosis?

Even though it is difficult to admit, when I looked more closely, my love appeared more to me like DIY crafts than fine art! Certainly, there were many times that I said "I love you" with great sincerity, but, today, that same sincerity leads me to doubt the clarity of those "I love you." "There are shadows in 'I love you.' Not just love, not just that. Traces of time spent . . . There is a contract in these words! Know that I . . ."[11]

I am aware that sometimes I got myself into things out of desire for the other person. Motivated by the newness, I would say to myself "we'll see" and, without conviction, "better something than nothing."

6:30 p.m. It was time for my meeting with Sabchu Rinpoche; time to start following the first thread.

Desperately seeking Susan . . . and me too!

---

11 *"Sache que je . . ."* Famous song by Jean-Jacques Goldman.
Translator's Note: Jean-Jacques Goldman. *"Sache que je . . .,"* by Jean-Jacques Goldman, Columbia, 1997, CD Single.

2. Interviews with Sabchu Rinpoche
I

First, I would like to say two or three things . . .

If anyone is wondering how a monk dedicated to celibacy could be legitimate on the question of love and relationships, I would say that monks are people like others
and that we are always in some kind of love relationship,
whatever the form, from birth until death. And as all emotions, including love, come from mind and monks are people who work with the mind, they know love perfectly. In
fact, it is the principal goal of meditation to access Love
with a capital L, in its unconditional form.

Every good meditator knows the idea of *I*, of **love**, and
of **you** because they all come from mind. The last thing I
would like to say is that, in our exchanges, we will cultivate the idea of two perspectives: the eagle's eye view that
allows one to have a broad overview and the worm's eye
view that looks closely at the smallest details.

In other words, the idea is to develop macroscopic and microscopic vision—two essential points of view for a complete understanding of phenomena and the situation.

Rinpoche, why is this analysis of "I love you" important to you?
Two thoughts come to mind. I would like to explore the phrase "I love you" in more depth with you because it is simple, and we use it so often that we miss certain things. That is why I think it is worth careful examination.

I think that I am not alone in wanting to understand this phrase!

Wherever you go—in any country, in any culture, in any language—most emotions and feelings that people express to those they love can be summed up in these three words: I love you. Everyone says, "I love you!" Gifts say, "I love you"—attention, smiles, parties, birthdays—everything says, "I love you." It is the essence of human nature, the elephant in the room, but nobody is paying attention. Like, "I love you," and the other person says, "Huh, what?"

The phrase "I love you" is the most concise, the most complete, the most powerful, and the most authentic sentence that we can say.

But, it is possible that there is space to improve the expression of this phrase, by understanding the functioning of the **I** in the **love**, and in our understanding of the **you**.

"I love you, my dear, my darling, my sweetheart." We have learned to say "I love you" from the very beginning. To our parents first, then our friends—our very close friends—then our partner, then our children. The older we get, the more, new understanding of "I love you" we gain.

At the moment of death, you can hear, "I love you, Dad." "I love you, my dear son . . ."

I think it is the most important phrase in our lives, that we use the most often, but it is the most misunderstood.

When you say "I love you" to someone in a true and authentic way, I don't think there is any problem.

But not every "I love you" necessarily means "I love you."

That's where the trouble begins . . . Things get complicated because the *I* has trouble with its ego, the **love** is tainted with emotions, and the **you** is subject to judgments and concepts. The combination of the three—ego, emotions, and judgments—forms an explosive cocktail on the order of a *sex on the beach*. That's the name of a real cocktail, right? What's in that cocktail?

"It's better not to know . . ."

[*Laughter*]

1. Who Is the I in "I Love You"?

So, if we go against the current, and we try to understand, Rinpoche! If we start to untangle the threads, what is this I, and how does it work?

Let's start by examining this *I*. Generally speaking, is it specific to human beings? If we zoom out and consider all living things, we can see that there are different kinds of creatures: human beings, animals, mammals, reptiles, insects, etc. Within itself, each of these animals nourishes a desire to live, to not be afraid, and to find the resources to survive—like food or the sexual relations for reproduction.

Does a caterpillar, an elephant, or a lamb have an *I*? From a Buddhist point of view, yes, just like a human.

The I *is a label that we put on a whole made up of different parts.* For example, if we make a building out of red Legos, we could make this designation, "Here is a red building." We could also attribute different qualities to it, but if we consider its true nature, the building is nothing more than a pile of Legos to which we have added the label *building.* This is how our reality functions. The *I* is very similar to this: a lot of pieces that—when put together—we call *I*.

Our body is a key part of what we consider to be *I*. Add to this our sense faculties with our five senses, our culture, our education, our beliefs (religious or other), our sexual identity, etc. All of these elements come together in an *I* and form our identity, our me, or even our ego—all these terms are synonyms. For example, you might say, "I am a French woman, a Parisian, or a mother, an author, looking for happiness; I have been through this, and I loved that or I didn't like this." These innumerable parts make up Isalou. The way we dress is also part of our identity, of course.

The same is true for me: the language I speak, where I come from, my gender—I am a thirty-four-year-old Asian man; Buddhist and frugal. All of these things make up my *I*.

And we identify ourselves strongly with this identity that we have created. The stronger our identification, the more it determines and colors our experience of the world and of ourselves.

All of these elements have become so important that we forget that they have nothing to do with what we truly are. If you look around yourself, everyone in the world is full of their own identity and what it means to them.

To remove all of these layers and discover what re-mains, we must travel into unknown territory.

In addition to all of this, there is another parameter; in order to be able to experience something, like our Lego construction, something else must be present to allow this experience. This is consciousness.

Consciousness has a fundamental mechanism, that of getting carried away by experience, of becoming absorbed in its own story. That is exactly what is happening right now in this moment. It is not a film but reality, and yet just like at the movie theater, we are taken in, carried away by the sounds we hear, the odors we smell, by the people going in and out of our field of vision—all of which we are constantly labelling. "Oh, what a classy guy," "it's hot in here," or, "it's cold," etc. Through our faculties, conscious-ness watches the movie. Because consciousness is there, you can enjoy seeing it. If consciousness were not present, we would be dealing with a cadaver in front of a screen. In general, when the consciousness is watching the film, it is not aware of itself; it is absorbed by the story of the film—and you are at the edge of your seat with the suspense and eating your popcorn!

So, everything we experience is like a film?
Yes, everything in our life is a form of representation, a kind of cinema in which we watch our own film. This is very important; take note: we spend our time watching our own film!

So then, we are just a string of images that, when put to-gether too quickly, we take for a movie? In that case, is

37

meditation a way of pausing on an image?
That is exactly it. You've got it. Perfect! We generally film movies at twenty-four frames per second, sometimes twenty-nine. In one second, you have twenty-four images, or twenty-four micro slices of life.

We are an experience with a body and a consciousness—a label placed on an aggregate of parts perceived as a whole, yes!

And then, there is another thing: at any given moment, you are like a mirror that reflects itself. Consciousness has the ability to be aware of itself. Our mind has self-awareness. The mind can focus on itself. And this ability of the self-aware mind changes the whole equation.

To go in the right direction, we can **already** ask ourselves, "Am I one or am I multiple?" According to our feeling, the *I* is whole, like the idea of the building we spoke of earlier. And if the *I* is in me, where exactly is it situated in my body? If it is *a single unit*, is it inside of me or outside of me?

But maybe it is multiple after all?

In the same way, where is the tree when we look at a tree? Is it in the trunk; in the branches; in the leaves? If we look closely at each part of the tree, we will realize that we cannot find this thing that we designate with the name "tree." We can see that it is only a label placed on something composite issued from nature. The more we search, the more we find layers. There is no end to it. Look at the evolution of the discoveries in physics. First, we discovered atoms, which we considered to be the smallest component of matter. Then, we realized that atoms themselves are made up of other components like protons, neutrons, and electrons. Then, again, we discovered that these most basic parts were, in fact, made up of other elements. There is no end to matter, in the same way that there is no end to mind. Mind is bottomless. [*Laughter.*]

I have noticed that this analysis leads some pessimistic people to the conclusion that **nothing has any meaning.** What is the point of all this if it is just a bottomless pit, and there is nothing there in the end? But there is not nothing. We only have to zoom out to find all of these things: protons, neutrons, then atoms, and then all of external manifestation—matter. Oof! I will not fall through the floorboards. The floor will hold me up; it is made of concrete, so I am safe! Otherwise, we might be scared to put our feet on the ground when we get out of bed in the morning! [*Laughter*]

I think the representation of an incorrect reality is very comfortable for us. We are so used to it that imagining another way of operating makes us dizzy and is even frightening. That is why, the more profoundly we look at this *I*, the more we become frightened to discover that there is no *I*! It does not exist in the way we feel its existence or the way we experience it.

If we follow this investigation through to the end, what is left, then?

Change! What you are is constantly changing. Continuity is an illusion.

Isalou has changed a great deal since her birth. We do not necessarily notice or admit this. We are like a teenager, responding to their parent's disapproving look at their outfit, *"You may not like the way I dress, but this is me!"*

39

If we listen closely to "**this is me**," we will notice that we have been endlessly repeating it for many years. However, this *me* has been changing all the time. I bet your taste in clothes has changed many times in the last two or three decades! And yet, we keep saying "this is me; this is me" without ever questioning this *me* or seeing that it has changed many times!

Think about a baguette. Do you agree with me that the slices could potentially be anywhere in the bread? Just like a slice of bread, we say, "ah, this is me," but if we look more closely, we will see that we could very well have been a different slice in the same bread.

I would like to go back to the film metaphor. What we see on the screen is not really there. The director makes us believe something. In the moment that we perceive it, we are completely pulled in and immersed in the story, and we love that! When the film ends, everything disappears. It was only our perception. But, so long as this perception lasts, we feel the experience that corresponds with this perception. Many things in our lives are a bit like this. It is like being in a dimly lit room. We perceive forms, silhouettes. Maybe it is an intruder! Immediately, our hand brandishes the pepper spray. Then, we turn on the lights and realize that none of it exists. There was no intruder. Because the intruder is not there, the fear also disappears. For the time that our perception lasted, we were afraid, and the fear seemed very real to us. This is how the *I* functions. We are so caught up in our reality that it seems unlikely to think that our *I* does not exist. "How could I not exist?" If the *I* does not exist, how can I feel pain? What is the point? Where do I go, then? We can see that this brings up many other questions. We must tread carefully here . . .

If the I does not exist like we think it does, then what is there?

Our buddha[12] nature is there. What is it? Buddha nature is present in each of us. It is our true nature: pure, spotless, clear, omniscient, and unchanging. It is simply a correct identification. As we said, the *ego* or the *I* is a mistaken identification, but this incorrect identification is so old that it has become second nature and is, therefore, very difficult to correct. But it is not impossible because each of us is endowed with the ability to correctly understand that we are, by nature, a buddha! The only problem—once again—is this incorrect identification. Therefore, it is conceivable to change—to correctly understand what the Buddha within each of us is. It is a question of identifying the sun rather than the clouds.

I know that when we use the term *buddha,* it is a little disconcerting sometimes because we think about the statue. We cannot help it. That is the way that we identify the Buddha. But if we consider the Buddha in terms of understanding, then we will have a better vision.

So, the Buddha is understanding?

The Buddha is understanding. That is a very good way to consider the Buddha. What is the Buddha? His statue? No! The person? No! But understanding, yes! Not in the sense that we understand that this drink is tea, but perfect,

---

12   Translator's Note: In general, in English, the words Buddha and Buddhism are considered proper nouns, as referring to a historical figure and a religion. However, there is no unanimity about the use of the word *buddha* in its many other contexts. I have made the choice here to reserve proper noun usage for the historical figure.

unsurpassable understanding. There is nothing superior to this understanding. You have understood, and, if you have understood, you have understood the Buddha. This is why, if you understand yourself, you understand the Buddha. It is very profound.

Therefore, it is possible to understand this *I* in a different way: by seeing that we are all buddhas. This *I* is, in fact, a buddha. The whole problem lies in our way of identifying with it. We think that the *I* and the Buddha are two different things, like a mug and a glass, when from the Buddhist perspective, they are the same thing. The difference lies in our way of identifying more with an *I* or more with a buddha.

Think about this understanding as being like the nature of reality. The nature of reality cannot change; it is fixed. What I mean by nature is the absolute understanding of ourselves and the world in which we live. This cannot change. If it changes, then it is neither truth nor absolute understanding, but rather relative understanding. For me, Buddhism is like a camera lens that allows me to look closely at absolute truth. I am what I am. Whether I look through this lens or not does not change anything, but when I look through this lens, at least I have a deeper understanding of what I am and how I am involved in the experiences of love and friendship and achievement. Today, love, friendship, and achievement mean something much more profound to me than they did ten years ago. This means that by using this lens I have deepened my understanding—and the journey continues.

I like the term "fully." To be fully aware. The state of buddhahood is a state of full awareness. Are you a buddha? No. Am I one? I do not think so. The goal of a Dharma practitioner is to be fully, totally, and perfectly aware. What is this like? How would we feel? I use everyday language—how would we feel—assuming that this state can be felt. I can only guess! I only have guesses. I do not have an understanding of it.

The goal is to understand that the Buddha and I are no different?

Yes, that is it! When you understand perfectly, you are a buddha! In fact, we just have to remove the impurities that cover up our buddha nature. It is as though your buddha nature were a dirty mirror. The dirt simply covers the surface of the mirror, but it is not part of it. We are in the habit of saying, "the mirror is dirty," but the mirror is never and will never be dirty! It is simply covered in dirt. In fact, we do not really clean the mirror. We simply remove the dirt. The mirror was always clean! This is why, in Buddhism, we say that everyone is perfect: everyone is a buddha.

Okay, but if our buddha nature is perfect, where does the glitch come from?

Buddha nature is simply a correct identification. By contrast, the ego is an error in identification. If the Buddha is perfect and we are buddhas, then how do we make this error? From a Buddhist point of view, the incorrect identification began a very long time ago. It is so ancient that it has become our nature. We have been through an incalculable number of lives, during which this error has been reinforced—so often and so well that it is now difficult to correct this error. But we have the capacity to understand correctly because we are buddhas. The ego is the Buddha; the Buddha is the ego. The only problem is incorrect identification.

I would like to come back to the word "glitch" that you used. When we talk about a glitch—an ego or an *I*—all of these things designate the same thing, according to my understanding.

Therefore, *I*—the ego, the glitch—is like a badly-behaved child who lacks manners, who is not very wise, and who has a lot of distracted thoughts.

Let's look more closely at the two most important factors that allow the ego to persist:

1. The ego likes what it likes. It likes something and, therefore, wants to possess it. The ego wants and wants again without end. However, it does not know exactly what it wants, as the object of its desire changes all the time. And it is so enormous, so unreasonable! This year it wants one thing; the next year it wants something else. We become real dictators! [*Laughter*] It happens!

2. The ego rejects everything that appears to it as a threat to what it wants.

In Buddhist terminology, we use the terms attachment and aversion. Attachment to what we are attached to and aversion to what we consider threatening. Everything that does not fit into one category or another is neutral. This is how a sentient being functions. This is the way that you and I function most of the time. That is fundamental ignorance.

So, ignorance is not knowing that we function this way?
Exactly. From a Buddhist point of view, that is ignorance, and it is at the heart of our functioning.

What do you suggest for removing the layers that cover up our true nature and becoming completely aware, Rinpoche?
We have short, medium, and long-term solutions. The ego that tries to see the non-existence of the ego is a long-term solution. It is not the first step. To help ourselves, we first need immediate, short-term solutions to ease the pain—Band-Aids, balms. If you are hurt, you put on a Band-Aid. It is simple and quick.

There are also medium-term solutions, like different therapies. The long-term solution is to always, ceaselessly examine the ego—to look it in the face, directly in the eyes—without being dominated by it or trying to get rid of it. You simply try to see how you identify with your *I*. Then, you will know how your mind functions. The long-term solution is to meditate on the fact that the *I* does not exist. As everything rests on the belief that it exists, this exercise pulls the rug out from under your feet! However, when you start out in Buddhism and you seek help, we do not immediately tell you *"The ego doesn't exist. You should meditate on that."* The prescription given is not the non-existence of the ego because it is necessary for the process to be gradual, and it begins by sitting quietly to develop stability. This is what allows us to correct the error in the ego's identity, but it is not simple business! The goal of this first prescription is to make your mind manageable.

A Buddhist's priority is not to start from the exterior

and go toward the interior, but to go from the interior to the exterior. If I ask you to go to the center of the universe, it would certainly be difficult for you, as no one knows where to find it! On the other hand, you are the center of your own existence. Therefore, you begin with the center of your own universe, your own kingdom, of which you are king or queen!

The ego is an incorrect identification. That is the first point. It identifies itself as a separate entity, which it is not. The ego also identifies itself as something independent, which is, likewise, an error. It strongly identifies as existing in a very solid way. This is not the reality. This is what the Buddha tells us.

As it imagines itself, the ego is not made up of parts, but is a whole, a sort of kingdom without change that is independent.

In summary, these are the three attributes that characterize the ego:
- Permanent,
- Independent, and
- One.

Although it is quite the contrary!

Permanent means without change. You do not notice, or you do not admit it, but this *I* changes all the time. Your taste in fashion has changed over the last two or three decades even if you say "this is me" without ever questioning this *me* or seeing that it has changed so many times. Change is the natural state of things. Nothing remains permanent or unchanged.

Independent means that which depends on nothing else to exist. However, from the subatomic level up through historic events and everything we can imagine, we are all totally interconnected and interdependent. We do not exist; we coexist. Our own existence is impossible without the existence of others!

One is the opposite of multiple. The kingdom as the *I* imagines itself is not made up of parts, but is an individual whole. We perceive ourselves as a unit that is separate from the rest of the world.

We have this central nucleus, plus everything that we consider to be an extension of ourselves, and this makes up our kingdom and all that surrounds it. We want good things to happen to our kingdom, and we do not want to lose a single particle of it. We want a perfect castle, a fairytale. There is nothing wrong with this form of idealism except that it is not coherent with reality. The reality is that things change. Everything changes.

Change in the literal sense is defined by a moment that follows another moment. But the kingdom of *I* does not know change. In this kingdom, in a certain way, time does not exist. It is beyond our imagination. How could we paint a landscape where there is no day, no night, and no seasons? The kingdom of *I* is without change.

Even if we could understand the attributes of this kingdom, they are totally ridiculous because they are not in accordance with nature. I only have to say it for you to understand. Nature is change. Nature is not independent; it is interdependent. Nature is diversity, multiplicity—not a single, unique thing. But who could argue with the *I*? The *I* thinks what it thinks, and that is all! It is a dictator who thinks A, B, and C—period! Moving on; no more questions! [*Laughter*] This is the reason why there is so much suffering. This way of functioning is in total contradiction with the nature of things.

Now, if we look at how human beings act on a societal, individual, or emotional level, we see that our behavior is based on this illusion of the kingdom of *I*. We think that we are one, independent, and permanent. If someone else is happy, I do not see why that should affect my mood. I take care of myself; my happiness is my happiness. If someone is crying in Ulaanbaatar, I think that this has nothing to do with me, but that is not true. From the subatomic level up through historic events, we are totally interconnected, totally interdependent. We do not exist; we coexist. Our existence is impossible without the existence of others. Maybe I am heading too far into philosophical territory here—we might even say into the territory of reality, but reality is what it is. It is very unfortunate that we function in a way that is diametrically opposed to reality!

A person is the ruler of their kingdom, yet how can you guide them if they are unaware of this functioning?
Even though the experience of each individual is specific to them, and even though each queen or king is unique, nevertheless, a queen is a queen and a king is a king. There is a kind of convergence of conditions and tendencies. They are all rulers, and, like all sovereigns, they do not like to be given orders! They prefer to give them—to summon people at will and tell them what to do. Then, the question is whether or not the king and queen are ready to learn about themselves. Do they really want to know what they

are and what they are made up of? Are they ready to hear that the source of all problems and the origin of all joys and difficulties is, in fact, themselves? It is not simple to hear. Often, there must be something like an earthquake in your life, something serious that acts like an emotional or physical electroshock. This changes the situation so dramatically that you begin to question yourself and your beliefs and to see things differently.

It is very sad that we function in a way that is diametrically opposed to reality. The question is, then, "Why in the devil do we function this way?" We do not have any other choice but to question our way of being by asking ourselves why we act this way, how we experience the world, and what we identify with. Instead of pointing a finger at society, we should look at ourselves. Why do I think I cannot change? I *can* change! It is within my power! Changing the human species is, perhaps, taking on too much, but I have supreme authority over my own mind, so I can start with myself!

You have absolute power over your own mind. If you make an effort, you can make yourself happy. You have the ability. And if you make an effort, the characteristics of happiness and the definition you have of it can change and evolve. They can move from a level more connected with sensations and sense experience to a deeper understanding of the notion of happiness that is not a mere sensation, but a simple experience that is not momentary, but something continuous and perfect.

This is why we begin by being kind to the queen; we try to win her favor, to calm her a bit—she is so stressed! She feels as though she is never queen enough.

2. How Does the *I* Function?

How Does the I *Perceive the External World?*

The world appears to us in a certain way when we are sad. When we are happy, it appears in a different light. I do not mean that, all of a sudden, the ceiling beams start doing strange things or the ceiling suddenly becomes something other than a ceiling. Of course not. That is a concrete and fixed reality. I am speaking more about outer objects' influence on what we feel. The feelings that these outer objects inspire in me depend on my emotional disposition in the moment, on what I am feeling within at a specific moment. That said, "appears" is maybe not the most appropriate word.

Let us say instead: I have a different experience of it. Experiences are, in fact, projections, as we experience what we project. If you project something pleasant on a painful experience, you may experience it in a pleasant way. Or, by contrast, we can experience pleasure as painful. In this case, projections are what we make them. For example, the projection of beauty depends on a multitude of components that have to fulfill certain criteria. When a phenomenon checks all the necessary boxes, then we experience beauty. If we see something that does not fulfill these criteria, the experience of beauty does not arise. Therefore, projections and experiences are closely linked.

Can you elaborate on what you mean by "projection"?

When you identify yourself with an ego with attachment and aversion, then the world you see—the reality you perceive—is a projection. Do you follow?

I am the projector, and this is my projection. I project my attachment and my aversion. Therefore, the projection is very similar to what I am. To give you an image: if you are someone with fierce hatred, you will tend to see people as being like yourself, as people with a lot of hatred.

On the other hand, if you are a person endowed with great compassion, the people you encounter will all appear very kind. There is a link between who you are, the people you encounter, and the world you live in. It is a very strong link.

People who meditate a lot seem to find a form of peace even amidst great chaos. By contrast, people who are very chaotic within can find themselves in chaos even when everything is peaceful. There is a real relationship between the projection and the projector.

There is a collective reality that we all share in which the sun sets for me just as it sets for you. Within this collective reality, if I say that the sun does not set, then I am wrong. However, the beauty of the sunset or the meaning that I give it is not part of a collective reality, but rather a part of my subjective reality. One day, we feel very good and, based on these conditions, the sunset seems magnificent to us. But the day we have a broken heart, we are indifferent to the sunset. There are many people in the world for whom a sunset is nothing more than that: a setting sun without any romantic projection. Some cultures ascribe a certain meaning to the sunset, and some people consider them especially beautiful because these people have this subjective reality.

Another example: if an impoverished family in India does not have electricity, and they use candles for light in

51

the evening, there is nothing romantic about this for them. In a country where electricity is abundant, lighting candles is considered romantic! A candle is neither romantic nor unromantic; it is simply a candle that is lit and that lights a space. Nonetheless, people maintain a great number of projections on the subject.

We are the source of everything that we project. That is what a representation is. Filmmakers exploit this emotional disposition—this weakness—in film to give their work meaning. The purpose could be to entertain or to deliver a message, but, ultimately, the film must come to an end. When you have finished watching, you must understand that you have received a message: that there isn't one! It is sad, but that is the reality. There is nothing; everything is our projection.

There is the projector and then the film reel. On this film reel, there are forms—a dance or a drama. If you like dance, the film can represent something desirable. In the second case, if you do not like dramas, then it will represent something unpleasant. Aversion and attachment operate on our projections in a very subtle way.

Consider the example of romantic relationships. You have a lot of different projections about what love is. Love is a prince on a noble steed. That is a projection. Your partner is a bit overweight and cannot mount a horse—but, in your eyes, he can because he checks all your boxes!

But what is a representation?
When a child plays with Legos and makes a bunch of things out the pieces and then says, "Look Mom, it's a giraffe," as a parent or brother or sister, you do not necessarily say,

"No, it's not a giraffe!" You let them play, keep them company, and even admire their constructions. Children have vivid imaginations for this kind of thing, which you no longer do as an adult. You have moved on to more concrete things than Legos. You are no longer at this stage; you have evolved. However, if you look closely, only the objects of your representations have changed. They are no longer Legos; you have simply replaced them with other things.

Take, for example, the heart emoji that is omnipresent in romantic text messages. What is it, really? Just a shape! Nonetheless, with time, we have become conditioned to find meaning in this shape, and it becomes what we project on it.

It becomes so important in our eyes that we can no longer say that it is meaningless. So long as this conditioning remains enjoyable, there is no point in destroying it. Even though the shape has no meaning in-and-of itself, it now has a subjective meaning.

Habitually, we are unaware that the foundation of our experience has not really changed. We think that we have moved on, that we are adults, and we no longer play with Legos. We forget that, indeed, we continue to play!

What are your final thoughts on representation; is everything we experience a representation?
Yes, we can say that everything in our life is a form of representation, a kind of movie theater where we watch our own film. This is precisely why I like images and film. I like the direct experience. I like working with something that is not intellectual. It carries a message without the

use of language. In other words, I like direct images and actions, which are their own form of language.

On the subject of evaluation . . .

What are the most important things in your life? For some people, it is their career, for others, it is partying. Each person prizes different things in life according to their representations.

If you are Christian, there is a good chance that your representation is that you must suffer for God. If you are atheist, your evaluation of life might go towards, "What is the point of that? If you're dead, you're dead. There is no God. There's nothing, so enjoy yourself; have fun; let's party!" We evaluate life according to our specific representation. If you are a meditator, you probably wish to stay in a calm and peaceful place to meditate. That is what has value for you.

Essentially, there are many different ways to evaluate life according to our own representations.

The most developed ability humans have is our capacity to evaluate and judge information that we receive through our senses. This ability allows us to identify what we consider to be happiness and good. Our desire is not only limited to food and reproduction. It is much vaster. We wish for fame; we seek security; we want to be nourished, but not only for the next meal. Despite ourselves, we evaluate every situation we encounter according to what it can bring us—or not—in terms of happiness.

This is the basis of our *I*—our ground floor, in a way. From this perspective, everything we do is motivated by the desire to be happy. Our definition of happiness evolves from childhood through old age because we change, but, in general, the desire to be happy remains unchanged. We try to build everything around this desire.

Is evaluation similar to ethics?

I hope that your values and your value system go with a system of ethics. If your value system is to kill one hundred chickens a day, then perhaps your value system is not very ethical. If your value system leads you to discriminate, it is not a very ethical system, but it consists of a value system, nonetheless. It is important to reflect on our value systems because they are very linked with ethics.

Consider a breakup as an example of evaluation. For some people, a breakup is not of great importance; for others, their whole world crumbles. Why? If the experience of a breakup is painful, why isn't it painful for everyone in the same way? Because, at the end of the day, the pain is not one hundred percent the result of the breakup. Our way of perceiving the events, according to a system of values and representations, determines a large part of the pain.

Clearly, I have very painful representations of breakups, considering what a mess I am!

You walk into Notre Dame and you see the stained-glass windows—real works of art! Have you seen them? It is very beautiful, and they mean a lot to us. One day, something happens, and the windows get broken. Naturally, we feel sadness. At this moment, we do not see the possibility of creating a mosaic using the broken shards of glass. If you look closely, in life and in nature, everything breaks. However, when something breaks, it becomes something else that is equally beautiful. We never look at things this way. We remain stuck on what is broken. In life, many things are like this: death, separation, disappointed expectations, or other unwelcome encounters and any events not of our choosing. And because these events do not correspond with our choices, we feel hopeless and upset with ourselves for not having control over reality, but we do not have control over reality!

In short, when something happens that is out of our control:

1) We get upset with ourselves.

2) We do not look beyond what is broken. If we are lucky, someone is there, taking care of us, and says, "Don't worry, there is something else beyond this. Look!" We wipe away our tears, and we try to look further, and we will see broken shards of glass that can now become a beautiful new work of art.

Then, the person adds, "Look. In life, in nature, trees, water—everything, goes through transitions and every transition constitutes a major change. Thanks to this change, the next phase is equally beautiful!"

This allows us to release, to let go of our blockages, and to create space. We let go of our disappointments and try to see the emerging beauty! I think this is what we call a positive mind. Not in terms of, "Be positive! Be positive!" How can I be positive by simply repeating it to myself? But if we look, we compare, and we see the facts; this is life, naturally, and nature is always beautiful!

Water is another good example. We drink water. We are made of water. Water fluctuates. It can be a solid or a gas, and it makes cotton balls in the sky, and then rain falls. There are so many different expressions and forms of water. Rivers throw themselves into the ocean. Water evaporates. It creates currents. All of these are just different forms of the same thing—including our bodies. If we look at our lives in general, we have been through many transitions, but we have not looked at these transitions through this lens. We go through them without knowing it. Accepting all of these changing forms, seeing the beauty in the transitions, and imagining the possibility of creating something new is the path that leads beyond sadness.

From the moment we begin to walk, we sign a contract that includes the possibility of falling. This does not prevent us from walking, yet the possibility of falling accompanies our every step. Walking and falling; we want one, but not the other. We seek one and try to escape the other.

On one hand, we are well aware of this. On the other hand, we are in a certain form of denial, believing that we will never fall. We imagine that we will simply continue to walk, but this is not in line with the truth. When we function in a way that does not take the truth into account, then sometime, at one moment or another, something unexpected will happen. The unexpected is never in the foreground. We prefer to leave it in a dark corner of the attic because, deep within, we do not want to believe in the unpleasant aspects of life, which are, nonetheless, real. We cannot wipe the possibility of falling off the board. Of course, I say this with great kindness toward the experiences you have been through. The question is the following: What defines Isalou? Falling is not what defines Isalou. What defines Isalou is what she does after she falls. Maybe she will dust herself off and keep going, like most people.

They fall, they get up, and they keep walking. Sometimes their walk is a little different; sometimes nothing changes, and they keep walking the same way they did before. Then, they fall again.

At some point or another, you will neither walk nor fall. You will simply stay standing in order to evaluate your way of walking. What is the ground made of? How do my legs work? How fast am I walking? What direction am I going? You will carry out the inevitable evaluation. In your case, it seems you already have. And now, you are walking again.

We must be patient with ourselves because we do not understand immediately. Other questions will come, and we must be patient with them too.

Does failure exist or is it a learning process?

Failure exists for those who believe in it. You are your body, which is a collection of physical parts. You are your perception, which is a collection of perceptions. You are your consciousness, which is a collection of consciousnesses. You are your experience, which is a collection of experiences. Therefore, you are all of these different collections.

Failure exists for those who believe that everything is binary, dualistic—who work in pairs of opposites. Failure and success; good and bad. Someone who does not believe in failure, who does not believe in a binary existence, who believes that everything is relative—does that mean they never fail? In the eyes of other people who see them and judge them, they experience success and failure, but I am not interested in the judgments of others. I am interested in what the person themself perceives. For, in the eyes of a person who does not believe in dualistic existence, there is no failure. Everything is relative. Everything is in relation.

Is this a good thing, then? In order to answer this, we have to ask ourselves who is asking the question. Who is this person? It is important to come back to the person in question and to ask ourselves, "Do I believe in the positive—a positive that is the opposite of the negative?" The answer will probably be yes. It is difficult to explain the essence of that which is neither failure nor success if we are looking at things through the lens of opposites. Yet, what we describe here is neither. On the other hand, talking in terms of success and failure simply brings us back to talking about the nature of that which is binary or dualistic. Does this sound philosophical? Yes, it does. Is it logical to have this discussion, considering that people believe in all things binary? Yes, of course. Left or right. You are at a fork in the road; which way do you go? Left or right? We constantly make these binary decisions. Should I ask this question or that one? Our discussion touches on the foundation of our existence. This subject is not all butterflies and rainbows, and it may seem rather dry in some respects. But that does not change that it is true. It is connected to the truth we are trying to understand. In trying to understand the truth, we also learn a bit more about ourselves, and we come back to the queen again and again. All of the answers always bring us back to the queen. Does the queen like these explanations about binary, dualistic things? Whenever someone asks a question, ask them if they like to hear about reality.

How can we develop step by step?

The first step of training is working on **no longer thinking that the *I* is the most important**, but recognizing that beings are all equally important. Your ego may ask, "But why?" The answer is simple: all beings have an ego, just like me. Therefore, we are similar. I get angry when someone offends my ego. Everyone reacts the same way.

Without being aware of it, you generally consider the people around you to be inferior. If you go somewhere, and you see people suffering, you experience compassion, but there is also a form of happiness because you are suffering less. Thus, there is a feeling of superiority.

Therefore, the first training consists in considering all sentient beings to be equal in their fundamental functioning. Just like me, no one else wants to suffer, to be hurt, etc. Becoming aware of this allows us to bring the rest of the world up to our own level.

After devoting time to this first training, it is possible to begin the second: exchanging self for others. **Compassion** is the logic behind this exercise. The ego is alone, whereas compassion includes all sentient beings. If a good judge had to decide who is most important, between a single person and all sentient beings, what would their decision be? Isalou—a single human being—or the billions of beings on the planet? The answer is common sense, but it goes against our natural instinct: "I am more important than others." Who cares if others have houses; the important thing is that *I* have one! I need a car, health insurance, security, stability. In fact, I need everything because *I* am the most important to me. This does not prevent me from feeling compassion for others, but it remains very limited.

Exchanging self for others does not mean giving everything to others. The idea is to open our hearts and our minds to others in the least selfish way possible. Indeed, the goal is not to say, "Look how much compassion I have for others! I feel good because I am among the *compassionate* people in the world!" Ego is central to this pseudo-compassion, and this is not the compassion we are talking about. When you practice exchanging self for others, the *I* is no longer front and center; you just think of sentient beings. To practice this second step of training, first you have to think that you are the same as others. Only then will you manage to conclude, "Sentient beings are more important than me."

Meditation is another form of training. In this exercise, we do not try to access the past or the future, but rather to remain in the present moment with clear awareness. The goal is to maintain this clear awareness in each moment. Meditation also helps us to separate ourselves from the experiences we have. When you experience pain, there is a difference between you and the pain. You are not the experience. The experience changes. Not being able to distinguish yourself from the suffering and, thus, becoming the suffering is more painful than the pain itself! The good news is that you can separate the two aspects. You are not eternally cursed! If you want to, and if you make an effort, you can look, practice, and progressively succeed in separating yourself from your experiences, which creates quite some space.

Isn't it kind of a selfish approach to focus on oneself?
Becoming aware of yourself, of what is happening in your

mind, allows you to see the outside as well as the inside of all things. Anger, or any other strong emotion, does not control you. Your mind becomes more malleable and docile. How? Due to this introspection. When we are no longer aware of what is happening, everything begins to degenerate.

The idea is to cultivate this power of introspection—of wisdom, of unbiased and aware reasoning—and to remain with it. Every decision that you make on this basis will be reasonable and in accordance with reality. Lack of awareness leads you to make the decisions that you regret most later.

Becoming aware of this allows us to begin to dissipate the illusion. This awareness is like a light that illuminates everything. Light banishes darkness in an instant. This is its very nature. In the same way, regardless of how long the darkness of illusion has been present, the light of awareness dissipates it in an instant. Even if you have certain habits in terms of your functioning, with continual consciousness of what is happening within, illusion will disappear, for it has no foundation to rely on. It does not correspond with reality.

For myself, I try to maintain a formal meditation practice. In addition to this, there is what I call spontaneous meditation. I do this when I am walking or driving, without any specific structure or prayers. It consists in cultivating this quality of awareness. There are also moments when I am not aware. Sometimes I am frustrated, intolerant, unpleasant, or unkind. Kindness completely disappears because I am not aware of myself. When we are aware, we make appropriate choices. We do not force our choices. They come naturally, and we do not give in to lack of reason. It is appropriate to be kind, helpful, friendly, etc. Without self-awareness, the *I* solely seeks out pleasant sensations for its own satisfaction and fulfillment. It completely ignores kindness in order to acquire this satisfaction. In this case, it is as though part of our field of vision is entirely blocked out, which prevents us from having a full view. By contrast, when we are able to see everything clearly, we accomplish exactly what is necessary.

It is possible to change the world, but we must first begin by accomplishing the change we wish to see in the world.

We meditate on this as well, of course.

We look inside . . .

#LookInside

3. Isalou
Offering!

December 21 marked my second-to-last day in Bodh Gaya and the end of the Kagyü Monlam[13]. Great masters; monks; practitioners—everyone was soon heading off to the various corners of the world to spend the holidays with their friends and family. Like a plant blossoming in the sun, I felt like I was overflowing with love from Sabchu Rinpoche's treasures of wisdom and from the kind smiles of monks of all horizons. My heart was huge and wide open. I felt tenderness for everything and everyone with no differentiation and no limit. There was a feeling of oceanwide expansion, of safety and unity.

---

13 Kagyü Monlam: A large festival of aspiration prayers for the wellbeing and happiness of all beings. Begun in the 15th century by the 7th Karmapa Chödrak Gyatso, the tradition continues uninterrupted through the present day in all of the lineages of Tibetan Buddhism.
Translator's Note: Kagyü Monlam refers to the aspiration prayer festival of the Karma Kagyü lineage. The Monlam carried out in other lineages are named for their respective lineages.

The next day was December 22 and my birthday. I love my birth date, with its two twos—I find it aesthetically pleasing and graphic! It is also the birthday of Vanessa Paradis (a dear), Jean-Michel Basquiat (a huge inspiration), Racine (the author of *Bérénice*, which was the subject of my practice thesis exam), and Pierre Brasseur (my hero from *Children of Paradise*[14]). In addition, I share my birthday with two longtime friends, Charlie and Nicolas. For the last twenty years, we have sent each other birthday wishes every year without fault. It is a vital ritual. And so, of course, the day is a party of sorts. I received a shower of texts, messages of friendship, special attention, surprises, and gifts—I felt how lucky I am to have a family, friends, and a lovely Facebook community who keep me in their thoughts, who spoil me, and who share their kind words with me.

I usually feel a habitual excitement at being the queen of the day. This year, moved by my exchanges with Rinpoche and nourished by all he has shared with me concerning me, myself, my kingdom, and *I*, I felt something quite different. I felt happy to celebrate it in a new way, in this legendary place surrounded by red-robed monks.

Curious to know how a master celebrates, I asked two Rinpoches—Sabchu Rinpoche and Dongsung Shabdrung Rinpoche—the same question, "What do you do for your birthday?" Their responses were identical: **"Offering!"**

Offering in the sense of making offerings—giving, but also offering of oneself; dedicating ourselves to others;

---

14   Cult film directed by Marcel Carné, also known for *Port of Shadows* and *Daybreak*. Translator's Note: *Children of Paradise, BluRay,* directed by Marcel Carné (1945; France: Pathé, 2012).

making ourselves available; expressing thanks. It is the complete opposite of the approach we have learned to celebrate our day of birth.

I felt XXL love for others and not for myself. It was a true paradigm shift: self-centeredness on one side versus altruistic love and generosity on the other. New inspiration! The idea was enchanting. I glimpsed happiness with a newly open heart, a possibility to give and to discover myself in a new way. This part of myself lacks some training. But isn't this the part Rinpoche tells me is the source of love itself? I made up my mind. The next day, I would wake at dawn and practice offering all day long—and we would see!

At five o'clock in the morning on December 22, the daylight was still weak and filtered. After a quick shower, I scooted down to the already buzzing streets of Bodh Gaya. I wound my way among the many pilgrims to meet up with Dongsung Shabdrung Rinpoche's attendant at the entrance to the market, where we had planned to go shopping for offerings for the Buddha in the Mahabodhi Temple.

Offering. We purchased apples, oranges, mangoes, bananas, clusters of grapes, bags of rice, flowers, incense sticks, and a magnificent yellow robe with a slight sheen. Then, this red-robed monk accompanied me to the foot of the Buddha's statue. We separated the offerings into three large bowls, and he guided me directly to the large, golden statue, where I placed my gifts.[15] I handed the shimmering yellow robe to another monk, who adorned the statue with it. As the robe covered the Buddha's left shoulder, I felt a great emotion. I had just offered a yellow robe—a robe the color of gold and the sun—to the Buddha in the exact spot where he attained enlightenment! Buddha was wearing my robe! What a historical moment!

I was so overjoyed to have begun my birthday in this most excellent way! And so proud of this new experience! It was unprecedented. I read somewhere that youth is a succession of "firsts." I had just managed to grant myself a little elixir of youth. But then: impermanence! Barely five minutes later, a second monk draped the Buddha in a new robe. And then another, and then another.

This outing set the tone for the rest of the day's good conduct. Indeed, we had better not get attached to what we offer. Once it is given; end of story! Only pure intentions and joy can remain, not whatever benefit we might wish to hold onto. I was really able to observe how letting go of all the tension connected to expectations liberated space for spontaneous things to happen, as though by magic. Being completely open—what a vacation for the mind and the heart! All day long, little unexpected gifts found their way to me, right up to the gluten-free carrot cake (nonexistent here!) that my friend Liz, who came with me on this adventure, carefully packed in her suitcase upon

15   Making offerings to the Buddha shows our appreciation and develops an inner attitude of humility, trust, devotion, and respect towards the diverse expressions of enlightenment— the dissipation of all suffering and the accomplishment of peace. Making offerings is both a means of training in compassion in order to attain this state and a way of accumulating merit. The positive action of generosity, motivated by kindness, produces a karmic potential that brings happiness and lessens suffering.

our departure from London and revealed that night with a birthday candle on top. Despite being a bit worse for the wear, it was the most royal birthday cake of all, for the queen of the day. **#Gratitude**, Liz.

It is also about making offerings with all of the people present around us. For the first time in my life, I blew out my candles with wishes of love and happiness, not for myself, but for others—for you dear readers. And it did me a world of good!

At the end of the day, I took a shower to wash off the dust. Beneath the water's warm caress, I felt a desire to go deeper, to clean more profoundly, to wipe away past hurts, and start fresh. I wished to open more, to give more in order to heal more quickly and to free myself from the insidious weight in my chest. I asked myself what the most difficult thing to give would be.

What came to mind was an offering of peace and tenderness to the one who had hurt me so. Not out of his wish for separation—after all, we cannot control the disappearance of romantic love any more than we can change it. No, I suffered more from his behavior regarding his newfound happiness, which was without modesty or discretion. It was humiliating and painful. I would have liked a courteous breakup, one that was respectful and kind and included the wish to cause as little harm to the other as possible.

On this special day, this painful connection felt to me like an empty suitcase—there was no point in carrying it around, and I was in the mood to travel light. Conflictual relationships serve absolutely no purpose in this life. They don't bring any benefits and they only bring complications for ourselves and those around us.

I got out my phone, and—heart filled with a full stock of sincerity—I sent him a text wishing him real happiness in his new life. This gesture, which I made first and foremost to open my heart to forgiveness, released a gentle sensation of serenity within me and gave me a new taste of freedom.

Making offerings is a seriously crazy approach!

Making Offerings to Rinpoche

I came to the end of my final interview with Rinpoche. In all, there were eight audio files of several hours each to transcribe. I felt a bit sad at the idea that our meetings were over. These conversations **on** love were real encounters of love—not romantic love, of course, but something beyond that. Immense gratitude toward Sabchu Rinpoche for all he had given me welled up inside me. Something was *happening* already.

"If I asked you to go to the center of the universe, where would you go? Where is the center of the universe? No one knows. But where is the center of your own existence? It is you, isn't it? So, we always begin with the center of our own universe: our kingdom. And who is the queen of this kingdom? You are the queen! So, begin with the queen," he told me with a gentle smile.

I felt a pinch in my heart as we waved goodbye in the cool winter night. The city was silent and deserted.

Walking home, two skinny little girls with large black eyes came up to Liz and me. One of them looked me right in the eye and rubbed her arms to show me that she was cold. Then, she gestured to the large navy-colored scarf wound around my neck. **Make offerings.** Without hesitation, I took it off and leaned down to wrap the shawl around her, rubbing her shoulders to warm her. I felt her thin body beneath my hands. Motionless and calm, she tenderly observed my care and smiled. Tears came to my eyes. This little girl and I were but one. I had become her, and the two of us, connected by an immense tenderness, had become all of humanity. After a few moments, she gently slipped out of my hands to go and shelter her friend under the wing of the large blue shawl. Together, they walked off into the deserted street.

"If you tame me," said the fox, "then we shall need each other. To me, you will be unique in all the world. To you, I shall be unique in all the world."[16] I watched them getting further away in the street lit by the weak light of the moon. They clung together, unified as well. From afar, they looked like two parts of the same heart, two open wings of a blue butterfly. Just before disappearing out of sight, they turned around together and waved goodbye.

Today, writing these lines, my heart is still full of profound emotion for them. Do they know they offered me the loveliest gift? Right up to the last minute of my birthday, they allowed me to express the most beautiful part of myself. How good it is to offer what we are to whoever comes and to simply do good. My heart is warm from something inside that connects me, that brings me joy, confidence, and serenity that I have not felt in a long time.

---

16   Antoine de Saint-Exupéry, *The Little Prince*, Chapter 21.
      Translator's Note: Antoine de Saint-Exupéry, *The Little Prince* (New York: Reynal & Hitchcock, 1943).

Midnight, rotation, the turning of the axes. Subtle trans-formation. A birthday entirely dedicated to openness and to the good of others allowed me to access a new dimension. I know it. I can feel it—something has opened. I look at the sky and thank the little blue butterfly taking me right to the stars.

It was one of the most beautiful birthdays of my life.

Gratitude. Then I returned to France.

LOVE

Paris, France
#Understanding and #Kindness

4. Isalou
February in Paris

February in Paris. It had already been two months that I'd been back in Paris, the capital of love, the city of romance. "Lovers walk under Paris skies. Their happiness grows on a tune written for them alone."[17] How many millions of people dream of kissing beneath the Eiffel Tower or in front of the Sacre Coeur?

Each morning, as I ran along the Seine, I told myself how lucky I am to live in the temple of romanticism. Each time I went out, I discovered new padlocks affixed to the bridges—witnesses to the lovers' vows of François and Caroline; Pete and Pavlova; Victor and Barbara. When I imagined all these lovers embracing with passion and promising each other "always," tenderness grew in my heart and filled me with fondness.

---

17   Édith Piaf.
      Translator's Note: Édith Piaf, *"Sous le ciel de Paris,"* by Hubert Giraud and Jean Dréjac, Columbia, 1954, Record. Kim Gannon wrote the English lyrics for this song.

In the morning, big snowflakes swirled down in a sumptuous ballet and took over Paris. In a few days, it would be Valentine's Day. These sparkling, light, little stars would spoil lovers with an added touch of romance. Love was in the air—and on the covers of all the magazines competing with each other to inspire us with their "Top 100 Valentine's Gift Ideas" and "200 Personalized Romantic Ideas for Him and Her." Armies of little red hearts had colonized the shop windows and streets. Soon enough, thousands of love letters, gifts, and sweet nothings would come to heat up the winter.

Internal Compass No. 1: #LookInside
Am I still in "egotistical-single-little-person" mode or am I in enlightened "me-loving-connected" mode?

Thanks to what I experienced in Bodh Gaya and the transcription of my interviews with Sabchu Rinpoche, a regular part of my days recently, I think I can say that my own little red heart is doing better.

"Each day is a new day for my developing mind and for the different relationships I may have because I am in the center of this, and when I evolve, they evolve as well. I progress because I am determined to progress, without letting myself be manipulated or influenced by what I experience. . . ." I have adopted Rinpoche's words and made them my own.

I am training like an athlete to progress and nourish the most beautiful dimension of myself, all while reminding myself that my ego is not the boss or the owner of who I am. My *I* is much bigger than this temporary little manager!

I am quite aware that my ego dominates me 99.9 percent of the time, but by being more attentive and consistently observing what mode I am in, I keep it at a distance. I think I'm starting to make out the beginning of a happy collaboration.

This consultation with myself acts like a surveillance camera for my conscience—like a tiny Jiminy Cricket[18] that says, **"Stop—look inside! Look inside! Introspection, self-observation, and presence."** In small moments throughout the day, whatever I'm going through with the people around me—my family, my friends, strangers on the street, in the Metro, in restaurants, shops, etc., I observe this little camera of self-knowing mind, as Rinpoche calls it. I examine with what part of myself I see, I understand, and I react. And, based on this, I readjust. When I'm having a disagreement with someone, I immediately ask myself, "What part of me is nurturing and pursuing this communication?" My stressed, impatient ego that wants to be seen, be right, validate or be validated, "Hey! I exist," or my kinder nature that listens and is attentive and generous?

It is practical and concrete training in a new way of being and acting in everyday life.

Plus, I am living with a new and important conceptual revolution: **I base myself entirely on the notion that we are our thoughts and that our life is the reflection and the result of them**. I already knew this. I agreed with it on paper, but that is one thing, while completely and totally

---

18   Jiminy Cricket is a fictional character, a small cricket full of wisdom who accompanies Pinocchio on his adventures. Translator's Note: *Pinocchio*, BluRay, directed by Ben Sharpsteen and Hamilton Luske (1940; USA: Walt Disney Productions, 2009).

integrating it into my way of being and acting and taking 100 percent responsibility for what I live is another. Since my interviews with Rinpoche, this truth lives within me, is a part of me, and accompanies me every day. It is a powerful structural change that paradoxically makes me lighter, as, finally, everything depends on me. If I trust myself enough, everything should be okay.

I have integrated the idea that the only way to succeed from day to day is through the work of *sculpting* my mind and giving it *good nutrition*.

To help myself along, I have summoned a new travel companion, a wolf from the Cherokee legend *The Story of Honorable Wolf and Harmful Wolf*. A grandfather explains to his grandson that, within each of us, there is a battle between two wolves. One is harmful; the other is honorable. The harmful wolf is filled with fear, anger, pride, arrogance, greed, jealousy, feelings of superiority and inferiority, of loneliness, pain, guilt, and lies. The honorable wolf is fundamentally good: joyful, generous, welcoming, loving, kind, honest, authentic, aware, fair, peaceful, supportive, and brotherly. He protects those close to him with generosity, attentiveness, and trust. Overall, the honorable wolf aspires to do good, while the harmful wolf is selfish.

"Of course," continues the grandfather, "it is difficult to live with both of these wolves inside, as they both wish to dominate our minds. The first wishes to do so while taking others into account. We call this aspiration. He makes effort toward his wish. The second acts based on his desires, looking for instant gratification without worrying about future consequences . . . They are both equally as strong."

"Which one wins?" asks the little boy.

"The one you feed," replies the old Cherokee sage.

"We are not in samsara. Samsara is in us, in our minds." Rinpoche said this to me one day. I heard it, it marked me, and it transformed[19] me from within.

Since then, I pay special attention to what I allow in, and I make greater effort to look toward others and at the beautiful and the good. I look for this in each moment and in all the little things in daily life.

The queen and her kingdom are learning to grow together. We are not shooting too high, but we are managing to avoid being painfully low. Sea level! That's not so bad for me, considering I was down in the abyss not so long ago.

My friend Marc told me that it's time I get back in the saddle; time to turn over a new leaf. He doesn't want me to do as he did and stay on the bench too long after heartbreak. I get the idea, but, for the moment, I am enjoying discovering myself more deeply—better understanding who I am, how I work—and gently nourishing the honorable wolf. I'll admit, desire and physical pleasure are kind of in sleep mode. No man enters into my personal space, and, in a way, it's like a vacation.

---

19   "Samsara is suffering. Buddha talks about the extremely subtle mechanisms of our mind, which change continually. All joy or pleasure that we feel—such as, "I like ice cream, so I am going to have some," does not give us any permanent pleasure. Maybe the first spoonful is delicious, so, of course, I want a second one, but at some point, I will not want any more; I will be sick of it. The final destination is always suffering. Can there be a real happiness that never changes? A permanent happiness? Buddha says, 'Yes. There is one. This is nirvana.' Nirvana is a permanent happiness. To find it, we must look at our own ego and see how we incorrectly identify with what we really are. We must return to the source and work on the foundation. In this way, it is possible to transform. This is the Buddhist perspective." –Sabchu Rinpoche

If I look carefully, maybe one man—a good-looking cardiologist that I considered surreptitiously—had caused a tiny, distant ripple in my stomach. I found it amusing that a specialist in battered hearts was able to make my convalescing one hum. During a morning of transcription, an idea came to me. What if interviewed this gentleman on the physical effects of heartbreak? For example: what is a broken heart? How do we heal it? I knew it was only a pretext for meeting with him, but, at the same time, the interview could be of real use for my work on love. On a whim, I picked up my phone. His secretary was out due to the snow covering all of Paris in a white blanket, and I found myself directly on the line with him. Though a bit surprised by my proposal, he immediately suggested a meeting that afternoon, in light of his many cancellations. Equipped with my big down jacket and snow boots, I braved the swirling flakes and crossed the city to meet him.

Between you and me, we clearly had chemistry. #LookInside. I entertained myself observing our dance of glances, our hushed voices, our heads tilted toward one another, our hands running through our hair, our smiles, laughter, listening, nods . . . It wouldn't have taken much for me to give in to temptation. Marc would have been reassured; I am not a lost cause. But, there was a problem: I didn't find this nourishing. This game of ego boosting, as my friend Charline would have called it, had no promise or importance. Certainly, it was charming, but it would end here. There was no need to go on or go further. Check-up; yes, it works. Confirmed. It was also a confirmation that this love-me-Tinder seduction mode was deactivated for an unspecified amount of time. At least, I hoped it was.

I think back to the little blue butterfly from the night of my birthday and to what I felt facing these tiny Indian girls snuggled under my navy shawl. I want to find this feeling as much as possible in my life right now. This experience showed me that my quest has changed its nature and orientation. The new one is so much more exhilarating to me.

When I went out again, I discovered that the snow had completely covered the landscape. The roads, the trees, and the cars had all vanished beneath the waves of white powder. Everything was fluffy and immaculate. The landscape looked as though it had been erased like a whiteboard.

It marked a new page of my story. I took a deep breath to fill my mind with the brightness and purity of the snow, and I made myself a promise:

On this first, newly single Valentine's Day, I bought myself a lovely ring. "You are gold," said the little paper that came with it. I quite agreed, and I was planning to bet on it! Once home, I sat cross-legged in front of my little altar, meditated for a while, and—having finished—made a new commitment. I put the ring on my finger like Carrie Bradshaw in *Sex and the City*. I said YES to myself, and I wed myself symbolically. I said YES to the queen! Not a declaration of self-centered love, but rather the celebration of a new outlook on life. **YES** to me who I will never forget again; **YES** to all the people who I will share the path with in one way or another; **YES** to this aspiration to offer the best of myself. Not when I feel like it, from time to time, or when I want to. No—all the time, from morning till night, through all four seasons, twenty-four hours a day, seven days a week, while trying to be more attentive to and aware of others because that is what does me good *inside!* Hand on the belly.

A permanent goodbye to my knight in shining armor on a white horse,

And hello to the blue butterfly!

5. Interviews with Sabchu Rinpoche
LOVE

1. What does it mean to love?

What does it mean to love, Rinpoche?

I think that love is complete knowledge of the other person. You know exactly how to identify them by their body, speech, and mind. You feel an innate love, and you care about them without feeling the need to prove that you love them nor to be physically involved. Your true preoccupation is for this person to be free of all suffering, without any judgment or personal interest. If it fulfills these criteria, I think that love is liberating, that it is liberation.

Can you call a tree growing, photosynthesis, and water meandering, yet always leading to the ocean, love? We could call the natural state of things love: interdependence, coexistence without the necessity of dependence, but that would be an unpopular concept of love.

The popular idea of love is something that is tangible; someone to talk to, to say that we miss, etc.

For example, water flows downhill, takes different forms, and has a natural cycle. Even if you try to intervene, it always returns to what it is and maintains its unchangeable character. **This is my universal perception of what love is**, but, generally speaking, love represents different things for different people in different places. It can also be one thing today, something else five years from now, and something different again twenty years later. But, in the end, there is an invisible connection that links one event to another, from end to end.

You have more experience than I do in this domain. It is possible that you are quite close to the reality of what love is at certain moments.

I'm not sure of that!
Perhaps if you are still not sure of what the meaning of the word love is after having been through many different things, then it is time to stop looking for love and start looking for the truth!

The chemistry of love is very difficult to measure. Everything comes down to chemistry. In the case of love, sometimes chemistry means attraction, but other times it is something quite different. Therefore, it is very difficult to know what love is made of. Sometimes love makes people stupid, and, sometimes, it makes them very wise. Love is a mix of chemistry and mystery!

Of course, what kind of chemistry is at work when we say, "I love you"? What is going on then?

Do you remember the eagle's eye view and worm's eye view we spoke about? Between these two is the experience of all our emotions. When we say "I love you" to someone, we are theoretically exposing our heart's deepest feeling. We are quite naked. We are saying, "I have feelings for you," and they are true feelings. In theory, we are quite sincere. If we consider romantic love—exclusive love— why do we feel this sentiment for a given person? We can look at it from various angles, from a psychological point of view or a social, economic, historical, or cultural one, but truly defining why remains a mystery. I do not know why we love exclusively.

On the other hand, Love—we can explain. Love is a beautiful feeling, a will for happiness.

Not in the sense of possessing someone, but of wanting total happiness for this person. This is what we find in love stories; we are ready to shoot the moon for the person we love to make them as happy as possible. We are prepared to do anything because there is absolute joy in wanting their happiness.

From a Buddhist perspective, happiness is a result, but we also wish to give **the cause** of happiness.

What does it really mean to love? People ask this question often! Why do you think it is such an important question? It is a sign, a guarantee that we all want love, that we want to be loved, and that we nourish an inner desire to take care of others. If the conditions are right, we like to take care of others and, in general, we like when they take care of us. To come back to your question, my sincere and honest opinion is that **to love means to take care of others.** It is an irresistible attention that manifests for someone, something, or a cause. Taking care of others; taking care of animals; taking care of the environment. It is very simple, but simple is easily confused with simplistic.

We need a certain degree of understanding of who people are, of the value of the environment, and of life in general, in order to develop this caretaking. But I cannot distinguish a love that is different from taking care. Taking care covers various facets: love, responsibility, etc., which are different names we give to care, but which all share the goal of making others happy. I can describe taking care in this way: dissipating or distancing everything that opposes happiness.

2. What is love made of?

What is love made of, Rinpoche?
Why don't we ever ask what jealousy and hatred are made of? They are likely made of similar things. The same ingredients make up all emotions.

Therefore, the question is not about love, but about emotions in general.

What are emotions made of?
We want to talk about love because this book is about love, but to speak only of love would be incomplete.

I think there are several aspects to an emotion. First, *I* is the core of every emotion, particularly strong emotions like love, hate, or jealousy. This may be the reason why people in love most often say, "I love you," which begins with *I*. *I* is the center of the emotion. "I love you. I hate you. Why is this happening to me? Why aren't I happy?"

Next, the second aspect of every emotion is that of winning and losing. We want to win, and we do not want to lose. Because of this, the *I* considers everything that supports its wishes as an extension of itself: my this, my that, etc.

There is the central core and its appendages that make up our kingdom and all that surrounds it. We want good things to happen to this kingdom, and we want to build a perfect castle without losing anything. In short, a fairytale. This form of idealism is not inherently bad except that it is not in accordance with reality. I change; you change; the particles that make up this table are constantly changing. My thoughts change. How can we be happy in a state that is not in accordance with reality? This brings me back to what I said in the beginning. If we really want to know what love is, then we need to know what ultimate truth is. Ultimate truth does not bring disaster or pain. The truth must be complete and not a collection of fragments. It must bring peace because that is its nature.

We are not ultimate; we are moving parts, as are our minds, all that we do, and the world that we live in. Our approach to others, to our ideals, and even to love and all the emotions that we feel must be in accordance with this. The problem arises due to this disconnect. We do not interact with the world as being ephemeral and in constant movement.

I understand your line of questioning, and I understand what people mean when they say, "I'm in love!" As the saying goes, "love makes the world go 'round." That is probably true, but it is not a guarantee of happiness.

People often say that Buddhism rejects emotions. What do you think about that?

Buddhism does not say, "Don't have emotions!" "Don't be sensitive." That is not the focus. We also sometimes make the mistake of thinking that emotions are bad.

We simply need to understand that emotions are not the nature of mind since we can dissipate them. For example, if we clean our minds well, we can dissipate attachment and anger.

If emotions are artificial in nature, then we can make them *disappear.*

More specifically, we can *clean up* our emotions and transform them into healthier qualities like compassion and wisdom.

Practicing on our emotions is like cleaning up the stains that we have created on our minds during numerous lifetimes.

First, we need to understand that the experiences of joy, pain, happiness, and suffering are rooted in emotions. It is also possible to deepen your understanding by looking more closely at the nature of the joy, the pain, the happiness, and the suffering that you experience. Understanding their nature allows you to feel free, almost as though you have been liberated from your emotions. This means that you feel emotions, but they do not affect you anymore.

What is the purpose of emotions no longer affecting us? There are various levels of happiness, from the most superficial—like chocolate or ice cream—to profound happiness, like seeing someone you love happy or the kind happiness of selfless altruism. The depth of happiness depends on the way you identify with your emotions in relation to the context.

For example, chocolate can make us happy. However, perhaps it is not simply chocolate, but the way that someone offers you the chocolate or the moment in which you are eating it. If somebody gives you chocolate on a day that you do not feel like eating any, it will not bring you as much joy. By profoundly examining the joy that you experience, you begin to understand that it is not only due to chocolate, but also to the way that you feel, the place where you are, and what kind of a day you are having.

All emotions function this same way: sadness, dissatisfaction, all of them! They all arise based on multiple elements. Recognizing this is truly liberating.

Our ordinary way of functioning is to accuse. If we are suffering from an illness, we will blame the illness for all of our difficulties. If we look more closely, we can see that cancer does not come from a single cause, but from many different things. It may be our diet, our age, our genes, the way we have taken care of our body and mind, the way we have treated others, etc. We no longer know what to accuse because everything is accusable. Not finding a sole origin is liberating. I think we have difficulty with this because there are many factors at work. If there were only one, it would be easier to understand.

Why do we experience emotions?
We have emotions because we have value systems according to our representations of what is good or bad. Based on

89

these representations, we experience attachment or aversion.

Why do we experience attachment and aversion?

Because we think we are separate. This is a major point. I am not this mug; I am not Isalou; I am nothing other than myself, separate from everything else. So, what happens to Isalou or to this mug does not affect me because I identify as a separate entity.

Does this correspond with the reality?

Buddhism explains that, no, this is an error.

Why am I making this error?

Because I am a human being who is not yet enlightened, and I have made a mistake. Seeing things in this way is not natural. On the other hand, what appears natural and obvious to us is our own feeling, according to which we are separate from everything else. Thus, this is what we believe. We do not question our natural instinct, at least not very often.

Meaning that if we follow emotion back to its origin, we arrive at the ego, correct?

Yes, it leads to the ego, the *I*. I am happy; I am sad; I do not care. All of this comes from the same source. When we transform the ego—in other words, when we identify ourselves correctly—then everything that arises based on this initial error no longer exists. Transforming the ego is not simple! We have our own way of relating to the world and to emotions. If the *I* is round and white, then the world becomes round and white, and emotions become round and white.

If the *I* is deeply attached to something, then we experience emotions of the same intensity as this attachment. If you are not attached to anything, you do not have any emotions at all!

What might that be like?

It is difficult to imagine because we function in another way, just as a fish does not know what life is like outside of the water. The Buddha described an enlightened world whose mechanisms, functioning, and workings are very different. We are unfamiliar with this world, but we can read about it, reflect, and analyze, and perhaps we can see the outline of what the Buddha spoke of. We can also try to meditate because our mind is very agitated. Through meditation, we try to help the mind become more stable and peaceful, which gives it a greater capacity for understanding.

The relationship between the *I* and the emotions is very close. According to the Buddha, if we transform ourselves, we transform our world, and our way of relating to this world will also be different. We currently relate to others in an emotional way. Most of the important decisions in our lives are emotions. Marriage—emotions! Have children—emotions! Divorce—emotions! Some emotions are instinctual, and others involve a little reflection.

Is love an emotion or a feeling?

I would include emotions within feelings. Feeling is a catchall word that includes even little feelings that are maybe not emotions. I would include all types of feelings. Love is technically a feeling—one that can be self-centered or one that can be selfless. It can be extremely varied.

Do you think there is a difference between loving and be-ing in love, Rinpoche?
I think the terms "to love," "to be in love," or "love" are simply different ways to say the same thing: to take care.

So, there is no difference between the state of love full of illusions and the fact of loving?
Who is the one who loves?

The agent involved is not the body, but the mind. The question we must ask ourselves is, therefore, the following: in our minds, are we really clear about what we want—our desires, our wishes—and what we do not want? What do we do to acquire what we want? Do the acts that we carry out and the words that we say correspond with what we want in return? It is important to think about all that. In general, this is not the case, but rather the complete oppo-site. We are very sure of what we want, but the acts that we carry out correspond with suffering, pain, and dissat-isfaction. Unfortunately, love begins with a very idealistic framework where everything is wonderful. Then, due to our mistaken way of being, our way of engaging with the other person and of loving them is imperfect. The emotion of love that we felt during the initial phase becomes some-thing different. It is not love that has changed, but there is a flaw in our way of being that distorts or threatens this love.

I think love is actually the victim!

How can love be a victim?
Let's imagine a scenario in which you find someone at-tractive, and you wish to be with this person. This ideal

attraction, like a gravitational force, remains like an imprint on your mind. During this phase, you are under their charm. However, we often forget that the person in question, you who are so taken with the other, as well as the world around you change.

Everything changes. The earth changes, the air changes, people change, and, more specifically, the two people in question change. You change physically; your taste changes; your ideals change. Despite this, you are deeply attached to the imprint of the initial phase.

In the beginning, perhaps your impression was quite correct, but time has passed, and the other person has evolved since, and you have forgotten to change in accordance with this. The initial ideal is not coherent with the current state of the two people, and a disconnect appears.

Instead of questioning our ideals, we often say, "I felt something in the beginning, but I don't feel that anymore," while, in fact, it is simply one of the systemic flaws that we face.

Can we discuss the question of lust? I find that in our cultural representations of love, there is confusion about what is love and what is lust, isn't there?
Yes! Because love whispers, and lust shouts. There are many things masquerading as love. Lust and passion attracts; it captures our attention. And attention is necessary to sell things. All of our society's marketing is based on the economy. We have to sell, and, to sell, we have to attract attention. We have to do this: [*Rinpoche claps his hands*]. The message has to be said and heard with force. So, advertising goes hard and heavy with everything that

attracts attention. A partially dressed young woman attracts attention. Even to sell cars, though is no connection!

Why does this work? Everyone knows how it works; we are all looking for passion.

Of course, there are some people who see beyond this, who do not become attached to this superficial view and who look at what is going on in the background. Some people say that there is something fake in what we see, and we need to look beyond it. In this way, we understand how it is constructed.

Why not directly sell lust, then?

Because lust has a bad reputation. And though lust is not love, we sell it as such, "Yes, yes. It is love. No, of course it's not lust! Believe us!"

We are often lost between desire and love. Can you make a distinction between the two?

The simplest way to understand the difference between desire and love is that love is free of all personal gain, of all self-centered will. Desire, on the other hand, comes from wanting something in return. Love is completely oriented toward the other person or persons. You do not play any role in the equation of true love, but you play a very important role in the equation of desire. If you take yourself out of the equation, the equation completely changes. The alchemy is totally different. I think that is the difference between the two.

I think that love may be desire, but love is more than just desire.

More than just?

Within desire, there is the idea of someone who possesses, who wants. It comes down to the idea of wanting to win. And love is more than that. Love transcends desire. If you really love someone, there is no idea of possession. Loving is not possessing but letting be. And if you really love someone, you are not the center of this love; you are in the background.

The person you love is in the foreground, and you welcome the background position with joy.

Love is the foreground.

Can we talk about attachment? What is attachment?

Attachment is grasping or fixing onto a moment, a person, a quality, or a place situated in the past.

Let's go back to the transitory nature of reality. Everything goes through phases and change. In an instant, you fall in love with someone, something, or a beautiful moment. You immediately try to acquire it, and it becomes an extension of yourself, a possession. If it is a flower, you pick it and make it yours. You do not realize that what you now possess has already changed. In this moment, you hold what was, not what is. This is attachment: you are attached to something without realizing or seeing that it changes.

Thus, the problem is not the other person, but you. If your approach to reality is in perfect accordance with its changing nature, then there is no place for attachment.

Attachment is a static approach to a reality that is in movement. Our static understanding or perception is true, but the problem is that it *was* true, some time ago, but it is no longer true. The thing or the person has changed, but not our perception. The *I* and the changing reality are so often not in accordance.

The true idea of love—not sentimental love—is to love from the depths of our hearts with an understanding of the changing nature of reality. Then, love is equipped with wisdom. Often, this is not the case, and love is nothing more than attachment.

How does this work concretely?

If both partners love each other with an understanding of the infinite possibilities for change that can occur for each of them and accept this change because it is the nature of reality—the nature of both people—then there is no place for conflict. Arguments occur because both people have a particular static impression of each other. Days, weeks, and months pass; many things change—physically, socially, etc., but, somehow, there is a subconscious, latent obstinacy that the other person not change. Generally, this obstinacy lacks the wisdom of the changing nature of reality. As both partners change, a lack of acceptance occurs because the static impression of each no longer corresponds with the reality of the other. This leads to arguments.

On a certain level, it is pretty unfair to expect unchanging behavior from a person in a reality where both individuals go through so many changes.

Attachment is **grasping** or **fixing onto** a moment, a person, a quality, or a place situated in the past.

Sometimes, love is nothing more than attachment, and, therefore, a potential for suffering. By contrast, if there is no grasping or fixation, there will be less attachment, and less attachment means less fear. Whereas, attachment generates expectations, and expectations block joy.

What are the different forms of attachment?
Life is full of attachment, aversion, ignorance, and ego. Where love is concerned, you can multiply it by two. Love is just a part of life.

Often, the emotion of love is not the reason a relationship fails. It is the incompatibility of the attachment, aversion, and ignorance of the two partners. Relationships fail because there are two people—two egos and two kingdoms. They do not fail because of love.

Can we discuss the topic of sex, Rinpoche? What do you think the role of sex is in love, Rinpoche?
A dialogue has a center and a periphery. If the discussion begins and ends around sex, then we can conclude that sex is the center of the dialogue and any extension of the conversation must be connected with sex.

If love is in the center, and we consider sex to be an expression of love in this context, then the rules of engagement are different.

That said, if this book is about sex, then I am not the right person to speak on the subject. I do not wish to be the Vātsyāyana[20] of the 21st century. Thus, I am happy that our subject is love, with all its various levels and aspects. I feel distinctly more qualified! [*Laughter*].

What is your process of qualification?
Love and hate, and all types of emotions, are manifesta-

---

20   Author of the *Kamasutra*.

tions of the mind. I have been training my mind for decades and continue each day.

This book principally discusses the essence of love (a microscopic vision) as well as its broader scope (a macroscopic vision). Based on our exchanges, it is clear that sex is not the basis for love, and love is not the basis for sex either, but, instead, the mind is the basis for both love and sex.

Sex is a sensation, a primary instinct. Love is not a sensation.

For many people, sexual relations determine the longevity, or even the validity, of love. In this case, sex is the lynchpin that holds the relationship together. Many people require both. For some people, one is enough. However, love and sex belong to two very different domains: love is an emotion and sex is an act.

Please note that there exists a love that requires nothing in return, including sex.

In what situation do you see sex without love?
Sentient beings—mammals and reptiles in particular, only need follow their primitive instincts in order to procreate. Evolutionary scientists theorize that they are trying to support their species. Dharma practitioners explain that, like all sentient beings, they are conditioned to act according to their desire, their anger, their ignorance, etc. Human beings engage in the sex act in order to reproduce, but also to experience sensual pleasure. In general, the idea is to give and take such pleasure with a person of interest.

And love without sex?
This is also possible. I would say that Dharma practitioners are supposed to be good lovers with or without sex. Once again, to understand the foundational ideas, we cannot stay on the surface; we must plunge into the depths.

Of course, on the surface, the principle of love is to give and take, and sex also fits into this exchange.

We live in a world where there is a book for everything: a book on hiking, on golf, on running track, on cooking, on raising children, on hairstyling, on sex, on love, etc. There are tons of books on love. It is a profitable business, but, to be honest, I do not think that it works. That is why there are so many books. If it worked, one book would be enough. If you meditate, you touch on a more profound comprehension of love that is based on a better understanding of yourself and the world.

3. Meeting the Right Person: The Good One!

How do we recognize a partner who we will be compatible with?
To begin, I think we need to ask the question, "What compatibility leads to meeting?" In other words, why do we meet?

From a Buddhist point of view, there is no explanation other than karma. What is the reason for Isalou being precisely what Isalou is: the way she was born, the path she has travelled, the mental states she experiences in this moment, etc.? We could say that she speaks French because she was born in France, but why were you born in France? If you trace each element back, you will reach a point where, either you are one person among so many others—a mechanical thing—or you will turn to philosophical suppositions and thus to karma.

To sum up karma in this context: a good cause produces a good result, and a bad cause produces a bad result. A neutral cause produces a neutral result. Our initial definition of "good" here is something that comes from a positive intention and that produces joy or happiness for others. If I give something beneficial to another person based on a positive motivation, and it brings them joy or happiness—even if the feelings are temporary—this cause qualifies as a good cause, in other words, a cause for happiness. A bad cause is the opposite of this.

In the context of matter, the result and its cause must coincide and share a common matter. For example, a corn seed will yield corn; a rose seed will yield a rosebush, etc. The seed shares a relationship with its result. This applies to all natural things. Karma is the relationship between a cause and its result.

We can divide the world into two: mind and matter.

Isalou's consciousness creates karma, and this karma produces a result. Past actions planted seeds, and they will give fruit. This is not directly verifiable. That is why it is a philosophical premise. As there is a law of causality in all that we see, there must also be one on the level of consciousness. If I practice meditation and mental calm for years, I am training my mind to become calm. By contrast, if I surround myself with agitated people and I, myself, am agitated, this environment will not bring me peace, obviously!

Thus, we are considering a philosophical premise:

Isalou is the person she is due to her karma. The same is true for everything she has encountered since her conception. She chose her parents, but not intentionally. It is the result of her karma.

Does that mean karma is behind every meeting?
Beginning from the moment when you take birth in a particular existence, you are tied to the laws of karma. At present, you are a human being. Until your death, you are tied to human karmic laws. As a result, your likes and your dislikes—all the things that makes you what you are— are connected to their own imprints. When you look at a whale, you appreciate the sight of it, but you will probably not spend your life with whales. Why? Because you are a human being. You are the result of your past acts, but you are also the cause of the results to come. What you are is defined by what you have done, and what you will be is determined by what you do now. This is the definition of karma.

Individual or personal karma is created by what you do physically, verbally, and mentally, without taking into account what others do. Collective karma is what you do with others. Consider an extreme example: if you kill someone on your own, it is an individual karma. If you carry out the act with a group of people, it is a collective karma because you committed the action together. The causes of a collective karma give the result of a collective karma. If you killed someone with a group, then the group of people involved will share the result of the collective karma.

Therefore, a couple's karma is a collective karma. There must be a karma with the consequence of the people you meet and with whom you spend time. This is not something that happens at random.

If a couple's relationship comes from a collective karma, what does it mean to meet? To share what?

We are dabbling in muddy waters here. I am reflecting on how to express things. I think the underlying question here is, "Is my life predetermined or do I have some control?" I think that is the starting point.

From the Buddhist perspective, both aspects are valid. Your life is predetermined by your karma, but, at the same time, your karma is not fixed. It is subject to change. Karma can exhaust itself, can be changed, can be postponed, etc. But who creates the karma? Me! If I want to create other kinds of karma or change the causes of karma entirely, I can do that because I am the author of my karma. The ego is the author, the creator.

This seems very philosophical, but if someone assembles all the necessary conditions for something to arise, the thing in question will appear—not due to your wish that it manifest, but because you brought together the conditions.

If a seed is waiting to grow, and the conditions come together, it will grow. It does not need your will or your permission for that. A relationship is very similar to a seed. If you bring together all the necessary circumstances, like understanding and various other elements, then it will succeed—not because you wish for it to succeed, but because you bring together all the conditions. The real question is not whether you have the will for it to succeed, but whether both partners ask themselves what unique, favorable conditions they need to assemble for their relationship to succeed. The key is not a wish for success, but a wish to find the unique conditions of success.

Every relationship is different, and each one involves its own unique conditions that belong to the two people involved. The responsibility is theirs.

Generally speaking, we are not aware of this mechanism, and we often consider what we receive and get out of the relationship, but not really what we need to bring to it so that it can grow with collective strength.

If you are in a relationship, is this due to karma? Yes, from a Buddhist perspective. Do you have control of whether it is good or bad? Yes, you do. How? This depends on what you bring to the relationship, and the way that you perceive things.

How can we best detect love from the beginning of the relationship in order to build something beautiful?

I think the real question is "How can I be 100 percent sure that what I feel is really love?" I think the first indicator is the feeling of love, with all of the definitions that we have already given. The second indicator is your behavior toward the person, what you want to do for the person. If you think your relationship should contribute to harmony in that same relationship and add to your happiness and you notice that your behavior contradicts this idea in some way, then I doubt that it is love.

What do you think of the type of meeting people call "soulmates"?

Every relationship has the potential to be a very important relationship. By that, I mean a relationship that helps us grow—a true, comfortable, real relationship, as opposed to a fantasy relationship that is some kind of fairytale with rainbows and unicorns and sparkly dresses. This world is made up of a ton of illusions that we maintain ourselves, so adding one more is not the issue. The soulmate is not the problem; the illusion is. The trouble is with the illusion.

And the idea of "the one"? Do you think that a single individual can be unique in someone else's eyes?
No. Every individual can be unique in our eyes, not just one particular person. Otherwise, it is like destiny. This notion does not overly bother me, but it is more important to create the best relationship possible, regardless of who we create it with.

You create your own soulmate over the course of the relationship, beginning with someone who was no one at the start. Soulmate means something along the lines of "the person who is perfectly compatible with you." But what does "perfectly compatible with you" really mean? We complete each other. How can two people complete each other? "He knows exactly what to do without my saying anything!" [*Laughter*]. But you, do you know exactly what to do for yourself? If everything is like that, then wonderful—life is great. But I think that is very rare and a little utopian, isn't it? This notion of soulmates exists in our imagination and in literature. It can be a good diversion for the brain, a good stimulant for the heart, or a little shiver in the belly, but do not expect more than that.

Work with what you have. You cannot work with something that you do not have. You must base your decisions on what is real, not on a phantom or a representation born from your imagination.

We always come back to this—illusion and representations.
Yes, always. The problem is not the partner. The problem is the illusion and the pain that the illusion creates. "Oh, I thought you were perfect, but actually you are not."

Whereas if you start with "I know you are not perfect, but I am not either. Is that okay? Okay, then let's get together," it is less of a fairytale approach and more of a real one, and real is good. It is good to begin a relationship on this basis.

From a Buddhist point of view, when we begin a relationship, we start by saying, "I have attachment and aversion, just like the other person." We cannot escape it. Attachment and aversion. I have ignorance as well, and so does the other person. If both people, together, have this same mutual understanding and the wish to grow together, then this becomes the incarnation of love.

"I want to grow with you." Choosing someone to grow with is very nice—we could even say romantic!

4. A Couple

noun:
1. two people or things of the same sort considered together
2. two people who are married or otherwise closely associated romantically or sexually

What is a couple to you, Rinpoche?
A couple is an agreement, I would say. A partnership.

This may seem a bit empty or perhaps non-romantic, but I think a couple is an emotional agreement. A husband and wife; two partners; a partnership. I would say that a couple is an agreement. It may not be very romantic, but I think it is an emotional accord based on obtaining something in exchange for offering something else, on an emotional, physical, or social level. If one party does not respect the agreement, sooner or later, it will be broken. If it is not completely broken, it will continue to exist in an imperfect, flawed way and will no longer have the same value.

What is a couple's mission? We generally think of it as a path to happiness, but is that really the case?
I think it is to be good to each other. That is the ideal mission of a couple. It is not a romantic point of view, but it is an honest and real point of view. It is not about happy days, but **days together**. As life is transitory, impermanent, fleeting, one of you will die first, so be good to each other.

In the world today, there is a very romantic image of the couple. I think it is an illusory version of reality. The reality is that we are not perfect. Nothing is perfect. Nothing works without effort. Everything requires investment—emotional, physical, and time. Just be good to each other.

The goal is not to be happy, but to grow together, correct? On a concrete level, how does this work?
If the two people in question are Buddhist practitioners,

the goal is to better understand what happiness is. There are progressive steps for this. Happiness, like all ideals, is a projection of the mind. Therefore, it is a question of developing an understanding of how our minds create these projections. The mind's ability to project things is truly fascinating. This self-reflection and self-awareness is one of Buddhism's fundamental practices. Therefore, a Buddhist couple should also practice it.

The focal point is finding the best relationship. Therefore, we must start at the beginning; in other words, the type of relationship you wish to have. Ideally, a good relationship is made up of two people who accept each other and who each wish to work on themselves. It involves understanding between the two partners, acceptance of the other's flaws, and the wish to grow together. This is a very good basis for a romantic relationship. With this in mind, you can love whomever you wish to love.

In the beginning, you think your partner is perfect—Prince Charming—and you throw yourself into the relationship. Then, you start to notice some flaws, and the illusion shatters. The problem is not your partner but the illusion and the pain brought about by the illusion. By contrast, if you begin by saying, "I know you are not perfect, but I am not perfect either. If you are okay with that, then let's get together," this approach is less fairytale and more real.

From a Buddhist perspective, when you begin a relationship, the ideal is that each partner knows they have attachment, aversion, and ignorance and that the other person does as well. Then, there is a mutual understanding with the wish to grow together. Choosing someone to grow with is very nice, and even romantic. It is the incarnation of love.

Can you define "grow" a bit more?
To grow means to see your own problems and flaws and to be ready to discover more and more about yourself with your partner's help. Each partner grows in their own right, but you hold each other's hand and grow together. Your partner helps you to grow. Instead of pointing fingers at each other, you can develop based on mutual exchange because the basis of the relationship is real.

So, growing together doesn't necessarily mean growing old together?
Growing old is a side effect, a byproduct of growing. Maybe it will happen. It is also possible to grow old without growing. Growing implies becoming a better human in every sense of the word.

Often, we leave someone because we no longer feel happy with the person.
I think it is incomplete to want the other person to make us happy. It is a very sad understanding of love and relationships. I think being happy is a side effect of relationships. For me, a relationship means growing together with intention. This means happy moments and other moments where you will not be happy.

Couples that have been together for over twenty years love each other very deeply without being ostentatious. It is a more discrete, more mature, more subdued form of love, but it is indeed love. Like everything on earth—trees, flowers, etc.—there are phases. If you ignore this, then you identify love with a single phase. This individual phase is as real as the others, but it will disappear. It will transform into something different.

As I already said, we change. Our desires and our aspirations also change. Look around you, and you will see that everything is impermanent and transforms.

Therefore, the number one problem is not appreciating the vastness of love, not seeing all the phases and transformations that nature traverses, and not seeing that you, yourself, are part of this change.

Wanting the other person to make us happy is oriented toward one phase in particular. Choosing this moment and wishing for it to last is an ineptitude that does not correspond with reality.

You can try to remarry again and again, but the problem will remain the same because it is not natural. It is a mistake.

If something breaks, then it is because we did not start with a good foundation, based on reality, from the beginning, but what role does impermanence play in all that?
I am interested in astrophysics and the idea of traveling to other planets like Mars. The rocket blasts off from Earth and then stays in orbit. The Earth's orbit has a certain speed, so the scientists must do many calculations of the speed and direction. They need to know exactly where Mars, the Earth, and the rocket are. The smallest inch of error and the rocket will miss Mars by hundreds of miles! I think life and relationships are a great deal like this.

In the beginning, we have a very vague understanding

of life. Thus, the whole mission is flawed. One person says, "I want you to make me happy," and the other replies, "No, I want you to make me happy." I do not see how this can work. It is a form of emotional slavery. Essentially, what the people are saying is "I want you to be my slave, and make me happy forever." This is a terrible outlook for a couple. This kind of basic principle with such an incomplete and flawed understanding dooms the relationship. The calculations are incorrect, and the direction is mistaken.

Impermanence does not prevent us from continuing to make decisions or from brushing our teeth. We cannot say, "Everything is impermanent; therefore, it is pointless to brush my teeth or have a partner."

Being in a relationship is not the problem, but we need to accept that impermanence is present every moment.

Generally, we only think about impermanence in difficult situations.

What is a good balance among my partner, love, my kingdom, and other people?

From a Buddhist perspective, when you bring an important person into your life, you do not only love that person, but you also accept a certain responsibility. A relationship is not only loving each other, but also understanding each other, and, on the basis of this understanding, adjusting as necessary. There is often a fixed pie chart: seventy percent for your partner and thirty percent for others.

In life, things are not generally fixed. Sometimes, your partner will get one hundred percent and other times only twenty. Each day is different, and you have to work out the balance daily—or even from moment to moment. Both partners need to have this understanding. It is what allows for an ideal balance: constant recalibration of the balance. It is not a fixed or definitive balance, but a fluctuating one. This tacit understanding makes it so that one partner does not complain and the other does not apologize or ask for forgiveness. There is a relationship—a form of exchange that is not obvious to the eyes of ordinary people but which exists within a perfect couple. That is the definition of a good balance.

What are the key elements of this recalibration?

We cannot constantly recalibrate the balance, not because there is a flaw in love, but because people are not always masters of their own minds. They are slaves to their egos, and they are shackled to them.

We are our egos, but we have the capacity to distinguish ourselves from the ego and to realize that we are not our egos. Unfortunately, the ego always finds a path in a sneaky and mysterious way, and brings us back to Point A. That is the source of the problem, not the balance.

The problem lies in a lack of control over the ego and a lack of understanding about the way it dictates our lives and, by extension, our relationships.

The king and queen have their way of regaining power over the ego's kingdom. Even though this kingdom only brings temporary pleasures, if it becomes the compass that directs our lives, it will not lead us in an appropriate direction.

It takes a cynical route that can be pleasant at times, with many detours, but that never leads to a stable and peaceful place. The problem does not lie with love, but in how the ego's strength leads love to evolve in a certain direction.

There is love and a sense of respect between a king and a queen. This love is not always colored by the ego's kingdom. It may be fairly pure. The error comes from not being familiar with the kingdom, as it is the source of this love. In the beginning, or on occasion, it goes in the right direction. Things are calm and pure, as they should be, but the force of the ego is such that it dominates love and leads it in other directions.

People who wish for a lasting relationship need to have a smaller ego. They need to be aware of the ego and have a certain understanding of its insignificance. It is not important that the ego always feel good. It is okay for my ego not to feel good. The point is to be satisfied with an unsatisfied ego. That is what really helps in a relationship.

Is it possible to develop the control over the ego that you describe?

My way of seeing it is that true control is based on ethical, clear, and wise understanding of oneself and the person with whom we are interacting, as well as appropriate speech and action. I consider this to be a form of control that includes a sense of responsibility. In other words, I do not act in an inconsiderate way. I control my interactions, and I do not do whatever comes to mind because my mind is at times a trashcan that produces a lot of garbage.

Maybe people are used to another definition of control, such as a description of obsessive or possessive behavior, but that is the opposite of control. That is merely territorialism. It makes me think of lions or tigers who mark their territory by urinating.

The kingdom of the *I* that has no self-control marks its territory with urine and the kind of control that means, "This belongs to me." Then it forces the other kingdom to abide by its own rules.

Life is certainly not only love. It is a mixed bag with many things inside.

What is there in this bag?

The bag contains many different things when we live alone. When we live with someone else, there are even more because we add their life to ours. Two people commit to each other and choose to live their very diverse couple's life together. They put their bags together. Some things do not change, but everything else is very different. It is difficult to know in advance! However, I truly, deeply believe that if two people love one another, that is the ideal, the essential, and everything else can be surpassed. Everything in their bags is not a problem.

As we have said, a lot of things in life are directly connected to the ego. There are a lot of *I*s that have never been diagnosed or confirmed (the spoiled *I*, the wise *I*, etc.). We often wish that life were exactly as we want it to be. We apply the same approach to love. Love is just one part of life. Life is full of attachment, aversion, ignorance, and ego. In love, this multiplies by two. Often, it is not love's fault that a relationship fails, but rather the incompatibility of the different attachments, aversions, and ignorances of the two partners. Relationships fail due to the two kingdoms, but not because of love.

You can help the other person for a certain time, but it is really yourself that you can help. There is a Buddhist proverb that says, "You can cover the whole of the Earth with leather because the ground is rough on your feet, or you can cover your feet with leather and make shoes, and it is as though you have covered the whole Earth."

The husband wants to cover his wife in leather. The wife wants to cover her husband in leather. But nobody wants to make shoes and wear them, and, in the end, they accuse love. It is pathetic. Everyone can put on shoes. It is easy and doable, but we cannot put them on someone else.

You want your partner to fulfill your needs. If they do, you can think they truly love you and say, "Oh, darling, you truly love me. You fulfill my needs. Thank you!" Thinking like this is not a problem in that you see a positive side of your partner. However, if you insist that they fulfill your needs, this is not the same thing and amounts to trying to cover them in leather. This is a major problem in relationships.

You mentioned living alone. What can you say to people who are sad that they are alone and have not yet found partners?
I would say that there is nothing wrong with you if you do not find love. I think that sadness comes from a feeling of lacking, of insufficiency. Why do people have this feeling? In fact, the only thing missing is someone to tell you that you are not lacking anything. "You lack nothing. You are not deficient in any way." In the beginning, this seems unbelievable because society tells you that you are only complete if you have A, B, and C. But, in reality, this

is not true. You can be single and happy. You can be married and happy. You do not necessarily have to be one or the other. Some kinds of suffering can be a launch pad to a better understanding of life. If the Buddha had stayed in his palace all his life, I do not think we would know of him today. He became the Buddha because he went out, and he encountered many different *you*—some who were suffering and others who were unpleasant and made him suffer. This suffering was his launch pad to accessing vast understanding, and, now, 2,500 years later, we are still talking about him. What he says is fairly direct and revolutionary. I hope to share some easily understandable and applicable aspects here.

5. How do we understand love?

What are the ingredients in love?
As I said earlier, kindness. If kindness is at the heart of all our actions, we will succeed in most of our undertakings in life. Being kind to oneself and to the other person creates a good foundation for building many things. We also need understanding.

I think that love is full of understanding and kindness. Understanding and kindness go together; they are in union. They are not sequential. We do not first understand and then become kind. I think that when you have love, you are spontaneously both. Understanding is kindness; kindness is understanding. That is very important.

How do you define understanding?
Understanding is like an epiphany; a realization; a reve-

lation. Understanding is when we are on the ground floor and not up on the third floor. Understanding is something very simple, as simple as breathing.

This understanding does not mean understanding the other person. That is not the goal of this type of understanding, is it?
We need to understand that understanding is kindness, and kindness is understanding. Kindness moves people because it is obvious, visible, but understanding is not. Others can naturally see your kindness, but knowing that someone understands requires assembling various elements. Seeing kindness does not require as many elements nor the use of language. Despite this, understanding and kindness are one.

Love, understanding, and compassion; how can we express these three things?
It is important to have love, not only for oneself, but for all sentient beings. Buddhism explains that if you understand everything perfectly, then you will automatically experience compassion. If you continue to move forward and you attain perfect understanding, then strong compassion will automatically manifest. This is the union of understanding and compassion; they are indissociable. Understanding is none other than compassion, and compassion is none other than understanding.

You said that compassion, taking care, and loving were really the same thing.
Yes, I used those different terms. The Tibetan term for compassion is *nyingje* (T. Wylie: *snying rje*), and the literal

translation for this is "supreme heart." The supreme heart is not the physical heart, but a profound understanding of the nature of beings' suffering and a will, a wish, for them not to suffer.

Buddhism explains that everyone wants happiness, and no one wishes to suffer. However, everyone experiences unhappiness and cannot find happiness. This is because we do not create the causes for happiness, but instead we create those for suffering. These are the words we habitually use: suffering and happiness. There are no other terms. We translate the word *dukkha* (Sanskrit: *duhkha*) as suffering or unhappiness. People understand this in different ways and attribute various connotations to this word.

Kindness, understanding, and compassion; are there other things to know to support a positive romantic relationship? Another essential point to understand?
Yes, winning and losing. If we take the eagle's eye view, we can see that the society in which we live celebrates winners. If you are a winner, no matter the field—games, sports, business—you benefit from special admiration. This same image exists regarding relationships. You can see it on certain occasions. Your friends send pictures of themselves posing with their kids and their friends in front of their beautiful houses, as if to say, "Look at how successful we are." This is the very essence of winning in the realm of relationships, the image of *and they lived happily ever after*.

A truly successful relationship does not necessarily look like that. I do not mean to shatter this beautiful illusion, but in a truly successful relationship, there are winners and losers, and some people lose with a lot of joy.

From when we are very young, society conditions us to win in every domain: a fight, a job, etc. This illusion of winning sometimes makes us forget the value of things. What is the value of parents and children, for example? Love. What is the value of a relationship between two partners. Love. With this constant pressure to win, we compromise love at times.

Imagine you have a horse. The horse has reins. When you are not riding the horse, you knot the reins to a hook. You could improve the quality of the hook, but its function is simply to prevent your horse from wandering off. If you pay a great deal of attention to the hook, but you do not feed your horse, it will die of hunger. In the same way, the most important thing in a relationship is to understand and nourish love. However, our training is to always win. In an argument between a couple, or a parent and child, everybody always wants to win. However, in the effort to win, we often trample on or neglect love. The habit of winning is with us every moment, and if we export it into our relationships, we will wind up trampling on the heart and, finally, destroying it.

What is the value of winning if it destroys the heart? You voluntarily let the other person win because the heart is more important. You do not let yourself get drawn into games. This is not a lack of courage, nor an ineptitude at winning. It is a deliberate decision on your part. You want to lose because the consequence of winning is the destruction of your heart.

Bombs and machines do not often destroy hearts, but rather insignificant acts that are a manifestation of the game of winning. If you want to succeed in a relationship, then be intelligent and protect the thing with the most value: love. Love does not grow on trees and does not appear accidentally. Love needs attention, care, and protection. Just as the smallest gestures make us feel loved and inspire us to love others, the smallest gestures can, likewise, harm love and destroy it.

We learn the game of winning and losing from the very beginning in life. Parents want their children to survive, so they push them to win. It is neither the parents', nor children's, fault. In Buddhist terms, it is simply what we call the eight worldly preoccupations: the hope of happiness and fear of suffering; the hope for fame and fear of insignificance; the hope for praise and fear of blame; the hope of winning and the fear of losing. This is nothing more than the expression of our way of functioning with the *I* at the center. I want to be famous and not unknown. I want to succeed and not to fail. You reproduce this same pattern with your child. They learn this way of functioning and, as they grow up, they begin relationships and import this game. Sometimes love suffocates due to this game.

Losing means admitting that our reality is not the most important?
If you choose to lose, then your priority is love over winning an argument.

From what I understand, being part of a couple means knowing how to overcome challenges and welcome change to make something new together. Is that right?
Yes, in an ideal relationship, both partners try to build something together. Something happens—the house falls

down—and you rebuild it. Maybe the house will be a little different, but you do it together. That is an ideal relationship. In a non-ideal relationship, the relationship would end.

What is the cause for ending a relationship?

There can be a lot of causes, Rinpoche! The desire for someone else, the desire for another life, the desire for something new . . . or boredom . . .

I think you touch on the essential point. We like new things. In fact, we like some kinds of change: changing clothes, changing diet, and, yes, changing partner. Being with someone for a very long time without getting bored is a very difficult thing for an ordinary human being with limited understanding of life and death. **On the other hand, if you like the company of boredom, I think you will have a good marriage.** This really comes back to what love is. For a person who can tolerate and even appreciate boredom, the definition of love is different. Some people don't like boredom and prefer adrenaline.

Of course, this is a generalization. It is also possible to like adrenaline and have a long marriage. But, in general, couples who have been together for twenty or thirty years no longer need "I love you" or sweet nothings to stabilize their relationships because, for them, the concept of love is no longer overly-sentimental. They do not need as much expression to support their relationship. They have known each other for so long that they can *feel* the other person from across the room. And they appreciate being apart as much as they appreciate being together. It can seem contradictory.

Can we say that this is a mature love, as opposed to an immature love?

I do not know, but it is certainly another level of understanding of what love is.

Do you think there are different steps in romantic relationships? We often speak about three steps. The first step is fusion with and idealization of the other: $1+1=1$. Then, we wake up and the second step is differentiation: $1+1=2$. I see the other's flaws; I return to my own friends and tastes, etc. And the third step is $1+1=3$. You, me, and us as a couple. That is the phase of construction. What do you think?

The overly sentimental love I mentioned earlier is probably close to the first step of $1+1=1$. I think the second step, $1+1=2$ (I love you, but I stay myself, you stay yourself, and we are different) is the flawed phase that we are all in during ordinary, daily life.

Everything would be easier if there were only one person. A relationship involves two people with two different minds and two different egos. One ego is already complicated to manage. Two, even if they are in love with each other, are even more difficult. Each ego's identity is so important that, even if two egos are in love, there is always some compromise that the ego does not want to make, whether it is in phase 1, 2, or 3. The compromise here is that of an ego that cannot accept making a new mosaic— as we discussed earlier—and still wants the same work of art it had in the beginning.

The ego goes through these three steps of love, even for people who are in the third phase. For a relationship to last, we need to be aware and understand the importance of **being satisfied with an unsatisfied ego**. That is what really helps in a relationship.

The closer you become to another person and the more you get to know each other, the more different the person becomes from you, and the more of a problem it becomes. The closer you get to someone, the more you love them, and the more you want them to be like you and not different from you. On the other hand, the early attraction existed because of this difference. Thus, because they are different, two people become closer, and, once they are together, the desire to be similar and not different emerges. It is pretty tiring, actually. Whether you are close or distant, in a romantic relationship or a friendship, so long as you are together, try to stay on the boat and afloat! Kindness is essential. Do not forget it.

6. Being Happy Together

Before talking about happiness, can we discuss the question of meaning and purpose, Rinpoche?
The human species is the only species that seems so worked up about the meaning of life. I do not say that with condescension. It is a natural process of reflection.

If I were an elephant and I asked my herd, "What is the meaning of being an elephant," I think the other elephants would reply [*Rinpoche makes the sound of an elephant trumpeting*] and continue to be elephants. If a flower grows on the side of the road, there is no particular reason for this, only that all the conditions came together: seed, air, bees, pollination or a bird. A lot of things had to happen—rain, the right temperature, etc. There is the flower on the side of the road. When the conditions come together, everything connected with those conditions can appear.

The subject of purpose is very important. If you make active decisions deliberately, with awareness and intention, and if you adjust and change certain things, then you give your life meaning, a goal. Rather than being swept along, you are the one who decides. From this moment, there is a certain direction—an orientation, a purpose—in contrast with the flower on the side of the road, which has no goal. It is accidental, fortuitous.

In general, we want to be carried. We ask, "Life, carry me. Carry me toward a better situation." No. Life will not carry you. You must carry your life in the direction of your choosing. This occurs in the mind, in your perception. If you act this way, you give your life a goal, meaning. Life is full of joy and love. We no longer say, "Look what happened to me," but rather, "Look what I created."

You are not on the receiving end. You are an active agent in your own life. Is there a better life than that? That is the best—being an active agent in your own life and knowing the how, the when, and the why of what you need. It is the most powerful and the most freeing thing.

This is not specific to Buddhism. It is simply a natural process. Of course, we understand it better thanks to the Dharma,[21] but you do not need to become Buddhist to understand this.

---

21 Dharma: Sanskrit term meaning "teaching." The Dharma is one of the three jewels of Buddhism: the Buddha (the enlightened one), the Dharma (the teachings), and the Sangha (the community).

What can you tell us about happiness?

Again, happiness is like all the other ideals. It is a projection of the mind. Everything changes, everything! It will always be this way. Eternal love seems connected to a culture or to mythology, in the way that many stories begin with "Once upon a time . . ." and end with ". . . They lived happily ever after." This type of story promotes a certain moral, but there is no guarantee. We choose what we like of the story and what we ignore. Generally, we like to focus on "and they had lots of children." We decide that this is the part we like, and we keep it.

Buddhism helps us understand that there is nothing constant. Change is the only constant.

Thus, there are moments when you are happy and moments when you are not happy. But that is okay; when you are not happy, there is the possibility of being happy again. It would be a disaster to be unhappy and to never be able to be happy again. That is not the reality. Depressed people have hope of no longer being depressed. They can get through it due to impermanence. Thank you, impermanence. It is not a sentence; there is no, "You will suffer for eternity in this state." From a Buddhist perspective, we have highs and lows. Because there are lows, there are highs. And because you are up high, there is always the possibility of falling. You can observe this constant fluctuation in the outer world and within yourself—emotionally, within your romantic relationship. It is the flow of all things, including relationships.

The problem is that we love the highs but not the lows. This attitude, this guiding principle, is flawed. When you launch a rocket toward Mars, if you aim only for the *bing-*

bing-bing—the highs without the lows—it will lead to disaster.

What is another way we could interpret "and they lived happily ever after and had lots of children" in Buddhist terms?
According to Buddhist principles, an ideal couple is two people who are identically imperfect, identically conditioned to make mistakes and be unaware and frequently lost, but who communicate, who choose the same direction in life, though not necessarily at the same speed. If one goes more quickly, they wait for the other to catch up without criticizing their partner for being slow. It is as though there are unspoken rules between the two people. A look or a touch is enough to express feelings and understanding between these two partners. They continue their life this way come rain or shine or storms, whether it is hot or cold, and they become disciplined at what they do. Then, one day, one of them will leave the journey first and die. Both individuals are quite aware of this and remind each other that their experience could end at any moment. One of them will end their relationship—not voluntarily but simply because they are conditioned by a human body. They will leave their body, and no one knows which of them will leave first. Both people are okay with this. When the day comes that one of them dies, can we say, "And they lived happily ever after"? Perhaps not, according to the usual definition of the expression, but is this happiness? Yes, I think so. It is not superficial happiness. It is happiness that involves contentment: being content with what we have. Both people are satisfied with what they have of the other and towards the other.

This is the story of a perfect couple. A perfect couple is imperfect. Both people know it and are entirely okay with it.

6. Isalou
Understanding and Kindness Are One

"Understanding and kindness are one. Though understanding is not necessarily obvious to the eye, kindness is. It is visible and immediate. It does not require as many elements, nor the use of words or language. Being kind is easy. It is accessible to anyone. Kindness moves everyone."

Ultimately, love is not as complicated as we make it out to be!

Following these last interviews with Sabchu Rinpoche, two essential points remain with me and blow my mind: kindness and understanding.

Being kind and thoughtful is less simpleminded than it seems. We can define kindness as "the quality of a person who shows benevolence towards others, an efficient activity capable of truly making others happy."[22]

---

22 Christian Godin, *Dictionnaire de philosophie*, Paris: Fayard, 2004.

"Be kind" is the first key to success in love. Thus, being kind is love in action. An ability to open the heart, a will to contribute to the other person's wellbeing—to truly offer them happiness and to accept them as they are. Which, of course, involves knowing how to let go of our preconceptions and critical judgments.

> **Thoughtfulness**: An attitude of the heart that consists of doing good and liking doing good.
>
> **Kindness**: Thoughtfulness manifest. Being thoughtful inspires feelings and acts of kindness. Being kind is liking doing good. Those who possess this quality are naturally generous.
>
> **Empathy**: Translation of the meaning of the Greek work *empatheia*, from *empathès*, which means "affected." Someone who feels deeply, who opens themselves to feeling. An inner ability to be in touch with others' feelings—without necessarily wishing to help them.

As Rinpoche says, being kind is also knowing how to lose sometimes in order to put love first and our connection to the ego second. That's another story. It is not easy to choose to lose when all we feel is wounded, scared, full of expectations, frustrations, distance: when our partner is not meeting our needs— when we feel that they do not give enough, they are not especially pleasant, they do not give us the attention we deserve, they are frequently grumpy, that everything is one-sided, and we are not seen, heard, understood, or appreciated. Basically, a major rough patch. When we feel like everything is dark, and we have completely reached the limits of what we have to give our partner, how can we find the ability to give and, what's more, the desire to do so? Stop, not possible. Dead end.

What I realize today is that, beyond contradictory emotions and complicated relationships, "be kind" **is truly** the little light that illuminates this new road through the fog.

It is a precious key opening the door to understanding.

Second key to success: understanding. This is the master key to the whole system. This ability to see with the heart and to feel the other person in a way that goes beyond appearances, beyond representations, and beyond complicated emotions that act as a veil means knowing how to go beyond the limited vision of our own ego, which only sees the other person superficially, and to use a different mode of connection deep within us that is subtler and more empathetic. It means already having gone on a journey of self-knowledge. It means not feeling different than the other person and understanding our own imperfections and inadequacies. This understanding is like a pair of infrared goggles that helps us make out the murky, subconscious functioning of the ego in action and the profound truth of beings that allows us to open our hearts to them—understanding and love intimately connected.

"Here is my secret. It is very simple. It is only with the heart that one can see rightly. What is essential is invisible to the eye."[23]

I had a revelation like a bolt of lightning when Rinpoche went into all this detail about understanding. Of course, how can we love another person if we don't truly understand them from within? I understood that we were not talking about a series of communication tools—useful, sure, like the *Ten Golden Rules for Getting Along*, the *Seven Keys for Transforming Couples' Communication*, the *Four*

---

23   Antoine de Saint Exupéry. *The Little Prince.*
     Translator's Note: Antoine de Saint-Exupéry, *The Little Prince* (New York: Reynal & Hitchcock, 1943).

Mistakes to Avoid, or the *Eight Pillars of Optimal Dialogue.* This meant a whole different nature of understanding. Deeper; more intuitive and generous; clairvoyant. All the tools in the world are not enough if we don't see the initial glitch of self-grasping and its mechanisms of projection that directly impact the other person and our relationship. For this type of understanding, we have to get to the heart of the system and relate to the other person using the right mode of connection beyond appearances.

This is precisely what was missing in my relationship with A. It was impossible to go beyond appearances and see the other's truth because we didn't have the right mode of connection and, on top of it, we were blinded by passion. In the beginning, we were fascinated by the other's universe, and this attracted us to each other. Then, little by little, as the sad story goes, the attraction turned into *tolerance* and then aversion. After the symbiosis and sparks of the beginning came the classic step of differentiation, during which we realize that the other person is not the ideal we made them out to be. The fantasy fades and the castle collapses. The result? A cascade of disillusionment, judgment, frustration, blame for the other's flaws, conflict, disenchantment, and eviction of the other from our affections. End of story.

It makes me think of a scene from a Netflix series,[24] in which two coworkers talk about their romantic lives. One, a clueless single guy, asserts to his married-for-many-years colleague that he has already been in a serious relationship.

---

24   *Call My Agent.*
     Translator's Note: *Call My Agent,* "Virginie and Ramzy," Netflix, 2017, written by Fanny Herrero, Benjamin Dupas, Éliane Montane, and Géraldine de Margerie.

"Yeah, yeah, I've been in a serious relationship."

"Oh yeah, for how long?"

"Three years!"

"That's not a serious relationship! That's a romantic comedy," retorts his colleague with a tone of mockery.

Rinpoche says that we are succession of experiences. I admit that I'd rather the final film of my romantic life not be too marked by this failed romantic comedy. In which case, it is worth it to do everything I can to understand, find meaning, and free myself from this experience in order not to go through it again. The violence of the narcissistic experience with A forced me to look even more closely at my patterns, my functioning, and my limits. From there, new paths appeared, like the idea of going to the ends of the Earth to find the keys with the help of a Tibetan master.

"I need a change of atmosphere."

"Atmosphere! Atmosphere! Do I look like the atmosphere?"[25]

I had to go to the ends of the Earth for a change of atmosphere and to find the keys with the help of a Tibetan master.

#LookInside and #Understanding

The third one's the charm, so of course I had a third revelation, this time with my friend Julia. Julia and I have

---

25 Famous retort given by Arletty in Marcel Carné's film *Hôtel du Nord.*
Translator's Note: *Hôtel du Nord,* streaming orange.fr, directed by Marcel Carné (2018; France: Imperial Film, 1938).

known each other for nearly twenty years. We have kept track of and taken care of each other through our various love stories, going from *cozy coupledom* to *chilly singledom*, then back into a relationship and back out again. For several years, she has been working on a PhD in Buddhist

Compassion: from the Latin, "to suffer with." Quality of perceiving and experiencing others' suffering and wishing to remedy it. The motivation of altruistic love to intervene and transform suffering.

Philosophy at McGill University with a thesis on training in compassion. While chatting on Skype about kindness, understanding, thoughtfulness, and all of these noble qualities one evening, she brought up new scientific research taking place since 2000 on this very subject.

It seems compassion is our first instinct. This famous fundamental kindness—a tad idealistic and taught by red-robed monks—is in fact our true nature.

This is a revolution of my fundamental ideas. We're not descended from millions of years of brute savages but rather humans who knew how to develop love, trust, mutual support, and solidarity to survive. According to this research, the survival strategy of the kindest is more powerful than the rule of the strongest. Our human nature is profoundly tender and sympathetic. And this time, it is not only Jean-Jacques Rousseau and the dreamy, gentle red-robed monks who say so but also numerous scientific studies.[26] Neuroscience, experimental psychology, comparative psychology, anthropology, and paleontology are all outposts of this revolution of our old ideas. What's more, I learned that Darwin, himself, the father of the theory of evolution, had already shown the importance of compassion.[27] It is clear that developing well-intentioned connections with others—as a mother naturally does with her children—is a better means of survival than relationships based on egotistical and aggressive struggle. That changes everything! On the one hand, there is a vision of society founded on cooperation, sense of community, and altruism, and, on the other, an ideology based on competitive, egotistical, and aggressive

> **Altruistic love**: Unconditional kindness toward all beings, capable of expressing itself at any moment toward each, individual being. A desire for all beings to find happiness and the causes of happiness.
>
> **Benevolent love**: The wish for all beings to experience happiness. Compassion focuses on the eradication of suffering.
>
> **Benevolent love and compassion** are the two facets of altruism.
>
> Matthieu Ricard. *Altruism: The Power of Compassion to Change Yourself and the World*. Boston: Little, Brown, and Company, 2016

---

26   Dacher Keltner's studies at UC Berkeley inventory a "compassion instinct," a natural, automatic, and essential response that ensures our survival. Jean Decety's research at the University of Chicago shows that even rats sympathize with another rat who is suffering and do all they can to help it out of its difficulty. The same goes for David Rand's recent research at Harvard University, which shows that the first instinct of both adults and children is to help others. Francesca Righetti of VU University in Amsterdam writes that, "Our first instinct is to help others," while Dale Miller's research at Stanford's Graduate School of Business shows the same, etc.

27   In *The Descent of Man, and Selection in Relation to Sex,* Darwin advocated for "the greater strength of the social or maternal instincts rather than that of any other instinct or motive" and suggested in another passage that the most capable are not those with the greatest physical strength nor the greatest intelligence, but those who learn how to mutually support each other . . .
Translator's Note: Charles Darwin, *The Descent of Man, and Selection in Relation to Sex* (London: John Murray, 1871), Ebook.

human relationships.[28]

"Cool breeze, morning breeze, breeze above the tall pine trees. Oh, the joy of the wind that blows; into the breeze, let's all go!"[29]

I understand better why we naturally feel such tenderness when we take a child—a puppy, a kitten, a chick, or even a baby hyena or shark, I'm sure—in our arms and watch them discover the world. Because they are vulnerable and fragile, and they need someone else in order to survive and build their strength, and this activates our profound nature of compassion.

It is so touching to know that this spot of tenderness and love we feel for them at this moment has its origin in this compassionate nature that we share within each of us.

#BuddhaNature

This leads me to ask myself a new question: **What if compassion and altruistic love are also the saving grace of our romantic lives?** What if knowing how to first connect

---

28   Why did our Western society forget about part of Darwin's postulations? According to Pablo Servigne and Gauthier Chapelle, the authors of *L'entraide, l'autre loi de la jungle*, it is due to a history of myths and to economic repurposing of the survival of the fittest. There are two primary myths that have been completely integrated over time and are now considered to be true by all without ever being questioned. The first myth: We consider war and competition to be the normal state of nature. The second myth: We consider nature and culture to be separate. We put humans on one side and nature on the other; man studies, controls, and exploits the natural world. For centuries, this cutoff vision of human beings has reigned. We no longer consider ourselves a part of an interdependent whole uniting nature, humans, trees, animals, and the elements in one family.
Translator's Note: Pablo Servigne and Gauthier Chapelle, *L'entraide, l'autre loi de la jungle* (Paris: Les liens qui libèrent, 2017).

29   Translator's Note: Traditional French children's rhyme *"Vent frais, vent du matin."*

our hearts to the altruistic kindness within each of us is a new way to learn to love the person who makes our hearts sing?

"Happiness created in the kingdom of egotism can only be artificial, ephemeral, and as fragile as a boat built on a frozen lake, ready to sink with the first snowmelt."
Matthieu Ricard's Blog

Internal Compass No. 2: Be Kind and Understanding

YOU

Toronto, Canada
#Caring

7. Isalou
"YOU" is Nine Pages Long

Despite verifying with the photocopy guy that he had, indeed, taken into account all of my files and that I had, indeed, given him all of the transcriptions, when he gave me the three envelopes of printouts, I immediately saw that there was a serious problem. "I" contained sixty-six pages, "LOVE," fifty pages, and "YOU," nine miserable pages. Should I laugh or cry? Did I miss something? Was this flagrant proof of self-centeredness?

If we evaluate the importance of a subject based on the number of pages we dedicate to it, is the *you* really that secondary? What if, in fact, this pathetic page count shows the propensity of *I* to dominate *you*? It comes back to representations. Do the *I* and its kingdom really take up all the space in a romantic relationship?

That night, my dear friend Charline came by the house

for an impromptu girls' night. We were both exhausted by our days and in need of relaxation and distraction. After sifting through the offerings On Demand, we decided to watch *Avatar* again with a light salad, a glass of wine, and a throw blanket.

When the Na'vi heroine Neytiri says to Jake, her love interest *"Oel ngati kameie,"* "I see you," Charline and I couldn't help being charmed by the declaration, and we toasted to love! Yes! What a beautiful notion! I see you; you for you; for what you are. I see you in your truth, in all your dimensions, rich with your past and all your experiences. I see you, and I welcome all that you are. I wish to take care of you, to give you the gift of my trust and the opportunity and space to be with me, free of burdens, masks, and fear. In the verb "see," there is the idea of perception, observation, and consideration—very helpful for choosing a good partner above and beyond representations, projections, and expectations. It is, indeed, you that I see, for what you are and not any interchangeable object of desire. I see you for you. That is a vision worth exercising.

During a period of my life, after facing cancer, I took up painting. It became a life choice. Like any self-taught artist, I wished to learn, learn, learn. Very inspired by Van Gogh, Warhol, Basquiat, Rauschenberg, Pollock, Bacon, Rothko, etc., I read tons of books on their biographies, their views on life, their aesthetic standards, and their relationships to their work. *Encounters with Bram van Velde, Interviews with Francis Bacon,* and Alberto Giacometti's *Why I Am a Sculptor* made up my evening reading. Giacometti taught me how to look. He is known for his paintings and sculptures of elongated, quasi-abstract human figures. His drawings, imprecise scribbles with uncertain shapes made of accumulations and an overkill of lines—of disorder, of mutations, of temporary limits—inspired me to consider the way we take in vision and knowledge of others.

He wanted to capture the presence of a being, and so he taught himself to see through drawing. Drawing to be able to see. The power of observation versus mental representation. An attempt to see by trying to get free from concepts and representations, by just concentrating his attention on visual information—contours, curves, angles, hollows, shadows, and lines. He worked on *seeing* the way we work on presence in meditation. Seeing with the mind's eye.

It is a lovely exercise in truth. I decided I had better work to sharpen my observation, to see like Giacometti, and to go beyond first impressions to better get to know and choose a *you*.

I see you. Walking through a dream, I see you.

With these words from the *Avatar* theme song in my head, I was sure that I did not see clearly enough, and I didn't know what to do with my *you* that was only nine pages long!

After discussing things with Rinpoche, I decided to catch a plane and meet up with him in order to go deeper into the subject with further interviews. Let's go see if I'm with **you**!

Mission: Pump up *you*! Destination: Toronto, the largest city in Canada. In the airline magazine, I learned that Toronto means "where there are trees standing in the water" in Mohawk, a dialect from Eastern Canada. In French, we call it the Queen City. I liked the idea of going to a queen city to meet a king in his kingdom.

The first evening, Rinpoche and I had dinner at a Japanese restaurant. I immediately felt as though I was with an old friend. Everything was filled with simplicity, kindness, and a sensitive and joyful listening ear, just like the Tibetans' famous gentle and luminous smiles. At the same time, as is Rinpoche's way, it was also invigorating and powerful! Watching the plates of sushi go by, Rinpoche turned to me suddenly and said:

"This sushi bar with its giant mirror and all the plates going by is like the functioning of our minds. Thoughts pass through our minds like these little plates of sushi going by. We have the choice to take each plate or not. In the same way, we can choose not to *grasp* what goes by in our minds. Can you imagine if your life depended on your choices in the same way as your choice of sushi? Take this plate or not; grasp or not. Vertigo!"

He concluded with a reference to Tilopa,[30] which says that appearances are not the obstacle; grasping what appears is the obstacle.

Worth meditating on . . . Indeed, it seems we cannot escape the clarity and strength of a wisdom master's observation even in a simple sushi bar!

On the way back to where I was staying, we walked side by side in the drowsy streets. Night had fallen. Silence and darkness began to fill the space. Only the moon and a few city streetlights carried on with their work. In Canada, streetlights are strung over the streets on electric wires, making them look like projectors at the theater or a concert. On the corner where I was staying, an out-of-whack

---

30　Tilopa (988–1069 C.E.), an Indian master in the Buddhist Tantric and Mahamudra traditions.

streetlight was blinking nonstop. "Disco in the street," said Rinpoche with amusement.

It was true that, considered like that—in this dark night with the flashing red, yellow, and green lights—we might have thought we were in an enormous nightclub.

I like Rinpoche's way of looking at things.

Beauty is an attitude.

I want to practice seeing as he does.

8. Interviews with Sabchu Rinpoche
YOU

Why Is the *You* Only Nine Pages Long?

Rinpoche, what do you think of the huge disparity in the number of pages between the I and this part? In a romantic relationship, the you *is as important as the I, isn't it?* In Buddhist practice, we never work on others, but on ourselves! We can never resolve problems outside of ourselves.

In addition, there are three things I would like to say.

Number 1: Every reader of this book is an *I*. You, Isalou, you are *I*. The reader is also an *I*, a husband or a wife—everyone is an *I*.

Number 2: The *you* is neither the canvas nor the stretcher of the picture we are going to paint. The *I* is the structure upon which we will draw a form, a landscape, a story—the *you* should never be the structure. It should be free, as free as a bird flying in the sky. *You* should never be locked in a cage.

If we work on the *you*, on the other, we do not grow at all! That is the problem in the world today. Everyone wants to teach everyone how to be, what to do, etc. That is not what we need to do! We need to teach ourselves. Then, you will become a better person—someone more mature, wiser, more informed, and more illuminating. You will become an example. Others can see it, and they will want to work on themselves as a result.

Learning about ourselves, improving ourselves, and becoming more inspiring; this is the perfect scenario! By contrast, the imperfect scenario is "Honey, you are not experienced enough, so I am going to teach you how to be and what to do!" This scenario is innate in some people, but it is neither the source of happiness nor enlightenment!

Number 3: If two lovers read our book, each on their own side of the bed, they will also connect it with their own *I*. When they close the book, each person will hold onto what they wish to of our ideas and choose to evolve— or not.

This book does not talk about the *you* because the *you* does not belong to us. We have no power over the *you*!

That is my approach. The opposite approach would be to delve into stereotypes and to project the *you*.

That is why there are so few pages on the *you*.

We reproduce this way of thinking in our romantic relationships?

Exactly. The *you* is not at all the center of the story. On the contrary, the *I* is the center. As every *you* is also an *I*, there is no point in worrying about the *you*. It also gets its fifteen minutes of fame!

Understanding the *You*

Who is you?

You is not me, but it is similar. Indeed, each of us has an *I*, so we are not so different from each other. This puts us on the same level. You remember, on the chapter about *I*, we talked about first becoming equal and then exchanging ourselves for others. To practice equanimity—in other words, thinking that all beings, including those we are in love with, are identical to ourselves, we need to put ourselves in their place. Doing this exercise allows us to see that they also have their own *I*, just as we do.

The person we are in love with also has their own "What about me?" Thus, there are two people saying, "What about me," and one insists, "No, me first."

The opposite of this is the first step: understanding the *you* and putting oneself in their place.

From a Buddhist point of view, in this life as in so many others, the *you* has been my parents, my spouse, my children, my enemy, my savior, my victim, my executioner. In this life, I am married to you; there is a marital relationship. If I am your child, then it is a parent-child relationship. If I am your neighbor, it is a neighborly relationship. The *you* can be anyone and everyone. From a Buddhist perspective, the *you* is a sentient being, like the *I*. In the same way that certain conditions and certain identifications created this *I*, the other person also has their own conditions, identity, representations, and value system.

And between the two, there is love.

Regarding love, *I* does not think it can love a perfect stranger. Thus the *you*, who gives *I* the opportunity to love

147

and to experience love. Thus, *you* is a source of gratitude and happiness.

You *is an object?*
Yes! Subject: *I*;

    Object: *You*;

    Action: Love!

    Without an object, the *I* cannot do anything, not even love.

Can you explain that further?
First, there is the context of a romantic couple in which the *you* is the loved being. Then, there is the *you* that refers to the family, friends, and everyone else. This *you* can be anyone. In every case, behind this *you* is someone who is not me. *You* cannot be me. If that were the case, if *you* were me, we would never say, "What about me?"

This shows that there is a distinction between *you* and *I*. "I am not you; I am me. Therefore, I need you to make me happy." This is typically what happens. Things function in this way because, as we have already said, we create a separation. "You are not me. I am me, and you are you."

From a Buddhist perspective, we say that patience is useful. How can we practice patience if there is no one we can develop it toward? If someone irritates you, that is a good opportunity to be patient! What more could you ask for?

Let's rejoice, then, to have the opportunity to practice often!

Yes! In conclusion, the *you* is absolutely not a mirror of the *I*. On the other hand, it can be a condition for realizing enlightenment—in other words, attaining serenity or liberation from suffering. Without *you*, there is no one who allows us to practice compassion or to grow. We grow thanks to others. Without them, it is impossible!

Is the you *only the sole object of the I or it is also something else?*

Let's talk about what we feel. I think that others have always been an object and *I* the subject. This *I/you* duality exists since beginningless time. Since our birth, *I* is *I*, *you* is *you*. The other has always been my object. This duality, "I do, and you receive," or, in the opposite direction, "you do, and I receive," has always been present.

In the ideal romantic relationship, the role of *I* and of *you* should diminish day by day to leave more and more space for *us*. I think we began our interview in Bodh Gaya with this idea. There is an *I*, there is a *you*, and, in a relationship, there is an *us*, a new identity. That is the ideal.

Is the you *a mirror?*

If the you is a mirror, the *I* is responsible for accepting what it sees or not. What the *I* sees is not always very pleasant because it is an exact reflection—like a mirror, which shows me as I am. This *I* is very important to itself; therefore, it needs to know itself. To construct a lasting relationship, it needs to know what it does well and the places where it makes mistakes. This opportunity comes when it sees itself in the mirror of the *you*.

"You were the one who wanted to know yourself? Well,

here you go! There are things you will like, and others less so, but it is indeed you!"

We can react in different ways, thinking "I hate seeing myself," or "This is the first time I've seen myself," or even, "I don't like you because you reveal myself to me. Go away!" The hardest approach to accept is the one that forces us to work on ourselves. Yet, this is what will make us better and more mature.

Everyone can grow, voluntarily or involuntarily. For a Dharma practitioner, it is preferable to grow voluntarily, rather than to wait for things to happen. It is thanks to this *you*, the person we love—be it emotional, romantic, or physical love—that we can grow.

Imagine a Person A and a Person B. In this context, A is *I* and B is *you*. Person A says, "I love you." For Person A to feel something—joy or sadness—they need to have a very anchored sense of identity, in other words, the *I*. Because Person A has a strong sense of *I*, **Person B becomes equally important.**

What is a good couple? Two people who are not only ready, but also willing, to be mirrors for each other—always with a great deal of kindness. These two people see each other, which allows them to see themselves at the same time, like two wheels of a car going in the same direction. Each is a mirror for the other to learn about themselves. This can be within a couple, but it is also true for any other relationship.

Love with *You*

Let's talk about coupledom. What does US mean and involve?

The *us* means including the other within oneself, with oneself. When *I* receives something, *you* is also there with me, and they receive something at the same time—or hope to receive it. However, it is not a north-pole-south-pole type of binary. So long as the other remains an object, the *I* will not give up their role as subject. The stronger the *I* is, the stronger the *you* will be as well.

Someone with a very strong ego can develop a very strong love, but maybe, one day, the other person will say that they can no longer accept the relationship. This love is too heavy, too rich, too quick, simply too extreme. The opposite is also true. If the *you* is very strong, the *I* will also feel this extreme aspect of the emotion. In fact, if the *I* and the *you* set sail in a relationship boat together and they both have very strong egos, the ship won't stay afloat because the two *Is* will be too heavy!

For love to appear—in this case, we are talking about wise and noble love—each person must moderate their ego and bring it back to a wise level. This way, the two people's emotions can truly connect them to each other. Otherwise, love will connect the two partners in the beginning, but a rift will quickly appear. The divide will grow until each person is separate from the other. This is often what happens.

This should be the starting point: I cannot make you change. You are you, and I cannot change that. If you are going to change, you have to do it, just as I have to change myself. If I try to change you, I will fail.

What do we do if we cannot change the other person? Change ourselves? It is up to each person to decide! If we want to grow as humans, we can follow through with the introspection that we talk about in the beginning of this book. This allows us to know what it is necessary to do and what we are capable of becoming. We gain wisdom simply by being aware of what we are, which has positive consequences for the person we love. Indeed, they will see changes in us, and they will see the energy we devote to this. That is the right way of influencing others!

When two people live together, they know each other very well, intimately. They know all the failings of the other person, and the things that were pleasant in the beginning are not in the end—like their habit of blowing their nose and not throwing out their tissues, for example. Knowing someone that intimately puts us in the position of judging, and we may be very surprised to notice our ease in doing so!

From a Buddhist perspective, this is an opportunity to discover something about ourselves. The *you* offers us this opportunity. The other person's way of being allows us to become aware of something within ourselves and incites us to change. "Hey, I didn't know I was capable of that!"

What do we do with this series of revelations? It is difficult to organize them. We are used to organizing familiar files in a certain way on the shelf, but what do we do with this totally unfamiliar file? There is no shelf for this one because it comes from within. This revelation allows us to see a problem. Now, we have to find an answer. Perhaps the answer is very beautiful and allows the *I* and the *you* to grow together as people. Each person growing is also both people growing together. Unfortunately, when we do not know what to do with these new folders, we react. This reaction provokes chain explosions, and then it is fireworks.

"What a blue! What a pink!" Then, things calm down—until the next explosion.

I think these explosions can be positive if we know how to deal with them correctly, but it seems too much to ask of an ordinary person, and society does not help in this case. Only books like this one teach you. Otherwise, we are missing a holistic approach, and we always use the same colors to paint the picture. A sunset is always orange, never pink, purple, or green. How surprising it would be to see a green sunset. Maybe this book will have the effect of a green sunset. The important thing is to focus on the sunset.

For the *I* to become a person of great quality—well-informed and wise—the *you* needs to be more important in the relationship. We are beyond romanticism here!

Be aware that I did not say the *you* would always be a source of happiness. There is no guarantee in this regard. It may be a source of happiness just as it may be a source of sadness. However, I guarantee that it will always be a source of discovery.

Definitely a source of discovery, and sometimes a source of disappointment. Do bad relationships exist? Of course, the I always needs to work on themself, but is it possible that some you are truly harmful?
Are you saying, "I take care of my side of the garden, but what happens if my partner not only does not take care of their side but also comes over and wrecks my side?"

Yes!
I have several things to say, but I do not know how to

bring them together, so I will simply share them with you.

First, you can contribute to someone else's change, but you cannot completely change someone. You can simply change yourself. That is the first thing.

I agree.

Another aspect that I would like to share: from the Buddhist perspective, we work on the *I* even if the *you* is harmful. As you just said, we always need to work on the *I*, but this does not eliminate your judgment, your sense of responsibility, or conventional knowledge of social norms. Individual responsibility—taking care of yourself physically and mentally (by meditating, for example)—does not erase what you think is good or bad.

It is important to protest if you are being abused, and you are doing everything you are capable of within your own social norms. It would be stupid not to protect yourself and to instead say that you are going to your personal kingdom to meditate if someone tries to physically attack you. How do you usually protect yourself if someone wants to harm you? You make an effort to avoid the situation and to arm yourself with various protections. How far can we go in harming others to protect ourselves? There is no definitive answer.

We have to appeal to our morals. What are your morals made up of? What are your ethics? Do you cause others suffering in the name of your own joy or protection? If so, is this ethical conduct? I think culture plays a large role in this aspect, as well as beliefs and socio-economic status.

Is the you a path to happiness?

Even if we need love, we like to be loved as much as we like to love and to take care of others. We might think that taking care of others is not a need, but if we observe ourselves, we will notice that we always wind up taking care of at least one or two people because loving and taking care of others is part of our nature.

Next comes the idea of compassion. In the first step, I need a reference point—a person to direct my compassion toward. **If you do not exist, and I throw a ball, the ball will continue on its trajectory without coming back to me, but if you are there, you can catch it and throw it back to me.** Therefore, it is important to me as a human and a Dharma practitioner that you exist and that you can be the object of my compassion. I am grateful for it.

In the context of the sentence "I love you," the *you* is very important because it exists. Thanks to the *you*, the *I* can reflect on its own qualities. How can I know that I am capable of detesting someone if I do not have the opportunity to detest someone? In the same way, I can never know if I am a good person if the other person, the *you*, does not exist.

Love, or any imaginable human quality, only exists due to duality, to things being binary. If I exist in a vacuum, no *I* exists. The *I* exists because the *you* exists. And because the *you* exists, the *I* exists, and because these two exist, love, hate, and all the emotions exist! These three aspects are so interconnected that we can no longer distinguish where the *I* ends and the *you* begins.

To come back to the question, it is very important for the *you* to not only exist, but also for the *I* to be able to take care of it, see it, and reflect on its qualities. This is important and adds value to my life.

Whether or not they do so consciously, the other person gives me conditions that I can use, material to work with. This is ideal from a Buddhist perspective.

Isalou is what she is today because of all these years during which she has been confronted with many *you* who have given her many conditions for growth. Here is the result: after twenty years, she has acquired the sum of everything she has received during twenty years of life. After eighty years, she will have the results of eighty years of meeting with different conditions. Other people, and not oneself, are responsible for offering all of these conditions. The *I* took these conditions and used them to grow.

What about happiness?

Happiness as I conceive of it is a smile, a laugh, contentment, or a feeling of fulfillment, of complete satisfaction. This happiness can occur on many different levels, and it always winds up changing.

The happiness we are seeking is an eternal happiness, like many novels describe: "And they lived happily ever after." Only, this is true in books, while reality, and truth, is change. What we imagine is not reality but fiction.

The happiness I am thinking of is not subject to change. It is immutable. I do not know what this happiness is, but, for me, it is the most ultimate happiness. I can call everything else happiness because there are temporarily magnificent moments, but, in the end, these moments change and are like suffering in disguise.

That is my answer to your question. It is hard for me to make it shorter!

That's not very romantic, is it, Rinpoche?

When you proposed the idea of this book to me, I first thought that this book was for you—a tool to understand something personal about yourself, like a sort of methodology. Writing this book on the basis of your own story, as I wished, will create resonance with readers that read the book with their own *I*.

The idea is to help their *I* naturally, organically, biologically, psychologically . . .

That brings us back to this famous idea of "organic!"

This book should not feed our illusions. On the contrary, it should shatter our illusions, break down walls to allow for cross-ventilation, and let in light. We have quite enough illusions. No need to add any more. A single lifetime is not enough to read all the books that explain the different paths leading to love with all the illusory ideas relative to each path.

I believe this book does not contribute to this accumulation.

By contrast, it tells the truth by adopting another point of view. It is an honest book.

Romantic love is very beautiful, but I do not believe that is our theme here. This book defines "I love you" on another level. We are not presenting the stereotype of love, but rather a different approach that people are not used to. I am not here to give them what they want, but rather to invite them to try a new type of salad.

"I'll have that salad."
"No, dear, today, it'll be this one."
"But I've never eaten that salad."
"Well, today, it's time for something new."

9. Isalou
Compassion, Big You, and Big Bang

Faithful to the Tibetan tradition, which closes every creation, teaching, or exchange this way, we dedicated our work together with joined hands, open hearts, and closed eyes. Thus, Rinpoche and I share with the whole Earth the merit we have accumulated while working for the benefit of all *you* through these transmissions, our discussions, and the business of writing.

"May this book be illuminating and beneficial for all."

We spent entire days exchanging and going deeper into our approach to love. Rinpoche sat cross-legged in a large armchair with a mug of cool water on one arm of the chair and his watch on the other. I sat across from him, in the same position, on a large couch, with my computer on my knees, surrounded by a mass of highlighted papers. From time to time, when I realized what I was receiving and what I would be able to share afterward, great gusts of happiness overtook me. I feel so privileged and grateful to have had these profound exchanges with Sabchu Rinpoche. These moments were truly enchanted interludes in ordinary life, during which I felt as though I were floating beyond time in a spacious, generous, and serene parallel world. There was life outside, and then there was the transmission that Rinpoche gave within the walls of the house. They say that when we are with a master, benefiting from his presence alone is a spiritual teaching.

One first word: Gratitude.
A second word: Breath.
And a third: Silence.

The day of my big departure, a beautiful spring sun was shining. We decided to wait for my taxi outside, against the little garden wall. Everything was calm. We could only hear birds and the distant buzzing of the city. At one point, we noticed that our favorite traffic light on the corner was still flashing compulsively. After a short silence in observation, Rinpoche turned to me and said,

"The traffic light we just saw is the same blinking of, 'And they will always live happily ever after!'"

We immediately burst out laughing, a common occurrence during our exchanges.

"Rinpoche, if we had to rewrite the fairytale ending," I

asked, "what would be the best way to put it?"

"And they **LEARN** to live happily ever after," he replied. *They learn!*

They learn. Big difference! **To learn**—my goodness, but of course. It is just the verb we were missing in those last lines of every fairytale! I took a video of the slightly wild flashing of the light to remember it by, and then my taxi appeared. We respectfully and affectionately said good-bye. At the airport, my heart was at once sad to be leaving Rinpoche and filled with immense happiness.

To learn. What it is really? There are ninety-nine synonyms in the dictionary, including assimilate, study, acquire knowledge of, improve, discover, integrate, memorize, teach oneself, adapt—and the last on the list, starting with the letter "w": work!

In French, the etymology of the word "learn," *apprendre*, means to take into oneself. To make knowledge one's own. How? By putting various mechanisms to work—like analysis, understanding, and memorization, along with a good dose of effort and a clear vision of what we wish to attain.

To Begin—Learn from the Past . . .

About the former *little you*, as uncomfortable and unpleasant as it is to admit it, you have already figured it out—I made a mistake. Even if I was looking for a life partner, an unfortunate internal switch led me into the arms of a prince, a twin, a mirror, a soulmate, or a savior . . . in short, a dive and another dive into romantic constructions primarily reflecting the idea of the fated love we are meant to find one fine day.

It is hard to build on a foundation of snowflakes . . .

I can check the box. Been there; done that! ✓

Learn to love solitude and aim for a 100 percent full bar of emotional self-sufficiency. This accelerates the process of strengthening the *I*. There is an important point to make about solitude here. In French, like other Latin languages, the world "solitude" refers both to being alone and to suffering due to being alone. Germanic languages have two types of solitude: one with a dimension of suffering and another that is purely existential. In German, "I am alone" is *"Ich bin allein,"* and "I feel alone" is *"Ich fühle mich einsam."*[31] With this recognition of the existential feeling of solitude that we all experience, we are better equipped to welcome it and even appreciate it. I had been in the arms of solitude for nearly two years. Up till now, I had been very frightened by it, but this time, we had a date. I didn't try to run from it. I didn't try to make it disappear. I didn't try to distract myself from it. I wanted to dance with it; embrace it; have a dialogue with it. I wanted to marry it, and I wound up taming it and loving it.

Then, strangely, instead of taking up all of the available space, it dissolved. In fact, I discovered that it was like the clouds of grasping and the illusion of self. Today, thanks to our dance steps, my bar of emotional autonomy is 100 percent full. Finding myself alone sped up the pro-

---

31   Translator's note: In English, we can distinguish between the words "solitude" for simply being alone and "loneliness" for suffering due to being alone.

cess. Learning to experience things alone—like going to the movies or visiting a gallery—allowed me to become more autonomous, happier even, because I wasn't trying to live through someone else. Now, everything that I can live with a *you* will be 120 percent! It will be on top, a bonus! Being good with myself and loving being alone allows me to think of the other person as an addition and not a completion.

Before, I think I wasn't full enough with myself; my battery only had 80 percent autonomy. Of course, what do we do when we are short some percentage points? We try to find them with someone else, without any discernment—"like a vacuum cleaner," as Rinpoche said. We enter into the dance of wants, needs, and expectations to fill ourselves, to complete ourselves. "Give me my missing 30 percent, 20 percent, 60 percent, please. Fill me." Loving solitude, in other words, loving **being with oneself**, is without a doubt the first project to tackle in order to be good with someone else. Personally, I give thanks for solitude; it has already allowed me to accomplish a great deal, to regain strength.

Learn to Surpass Your Own Confusion

I am well aware that I can only offer what I already possess. If I have clarity and joy within myself, I can share them nicely with another person. If, on the other hand, I have unhappiness, loneliness, and suffering, what do I have to offer? When we have love for ourselves, loving another person becomes obvious, so it seems. Our job in daily life is knowing how to surpass our own confusion and find the path of a peaceful heart. To help with this when I am feeling cloaked in a fog of unhappiness and like I've given control over to my inner harmful wolf, well, I hop on a plane. Not for real, but I think about all the times on a plane when the weather on the ground was rainy and, as the plane rose above the clouds, I rediscovered the luminous immensity of the sky—infinite and serene, crowned by a majestic sun. Where does the sky begin and end? It does not end. It is unlimited . . . and, as Rinpoche says, it is within us! We can surpass the ego's confusion and return to our true inner home—breath, calm, and joy. We've all had this experience of rising above the clouds in a plane, haven't we?

Reflect on and Develop Your Own Life Plan

The ideal is not depending on the other person to feel secure. Going back to what Rinpoche said: the other person has nothing to do with that. It is too great a burden to implicitly ask that they make us happy. That should not be their mission. Each of us has to find our own ability to be happy. We each have our own destiny. Even the most romantic among us know that, in everyday life, couples have to deal with issues that are less than romantic, like the balance of power, managing finances, raising children, respecting each other's space, and so on. Managing our own issues first is the only solution. Otherwise, we wind up forgetting ourselves—which can become even more dramatic if the other person decides to break the mold by readjusting their role or leaving the codependent little nest. *Boom*—at this moment, we find ourselves without a plan because the other person's plan was our plan.

In all the romances that go awry, we tend to hear this formula about how blame is equal: fifty-fifty. Oh, no! For me, now, that is over. The new rules of the game are those of the *I*, in other words, me and my ability to understand. Thus, 100 percent of the responsibility is mine.

Learn to Know Your Partner

Based on my interviews with Rinpoche, I realized that when two people say "I love you" under the pale moonlight (lol), it is above all the meeting of two egos[32] groping their way ahead with blindfolds over their eyes while balancing on a giant spinning top. It is an exercise in style more than anything else! Instead, let's prioritize realism and lucidity. First, he is going from prince to **partner**! We know that to create an organization or a business, we need to take time to meet with potential associates in order to discuss our visions and goals. In this context, it is better to be clear from the outset and know what we are committing to. It concerns our hard-earned money, our personal comfort, our security, and our ambitions. But why is it any different for romantic relationships? Being part of a couple is just as serious a job! Take note: it is in no way my intention to take away from the miraculous nature of meeting someone. I just want to take care of that connection.

---

32   Or two "unconscious minds" as psychology might say, even if this is not exactly the same idea.

Beyond being a **partner**, I also like the idea that he'll be my **best friend**. Friendship is doubtless a couple's strongest ally. This seems so obvious to me today, just as obvious as the fact that friendship is not in the **prince**'s job description. A prince gallops in on his horse to save damsels in distress or conquer new lands, but he is not a friend or confidant who will be there no matter what.

Learn to Build Together

I have a story in mind to illustrate this idea that inspires me today. I was part of a group of twenty people who got together. We were all blindfolded and forbidden to speak to each other. They sat us in pairs around a table. Between my mysterious partner and I, there was a pile of clay. The instructions were to sculpt something together without seeing each other or talking to each other—by only communicating with our hands. Understanding the other's wishes, getting them to understand yours, and creating something together was a serious challenge! Out of the ten couples at the table, only three managed to produce recognizable objects: a sun, a tree, and a vase. Like most of the group, my partner and I had not managed to communicate, and we had created something that wasn't anything at all. Some people had given up in anger, concluding that their partner obviously didn't understand anything! Even though it is not the case most of the time, it is possible to build something together. Even blindfolded and in tricky situations, it is possible. The possibility exists.

Each of us has our own construction model. I did some

research on various models, and I discovered the five marital styles, as defined by a team of sociologists from the University of Geneva.[33]

The Codependent Styles: Us against the world.

Bastion Style: Fusion, fusion—we are one and we melt into our us. We are united for the best and the worst in the hopes of growing old together. Long live routine!

Cocoon Style: We cajole and reassure each other often. We are alone against everyone else with a maximum of tenderness and support against the difficulties of existence.

The Independent Styles: Me first.

Association Style: Our autonomy keeps us together. We share the idea that we are happier together if each of us is in charge of their own direction. Down with routine!

Parallel Style: We are together because we do not know what else to do. It is not a party, but it could last a long time.

The Ideal Couple: Us and others.

Companionship Style: Yes, we assert our similarities and are bonded for life, but what sets us apart from Bastion or Cocoon couples is our strong participation in community involvement or humanitarian activities. **The members of this couple are model citizens.**

---

33 Sources: Jean Kellerhals, Eric Widmer, and René Levy. *Mesure et démesure du couple : cohésion, crises et résilience dans la vie des couples*, Payot.
Translator's Note: Jean Kellerhals, Eric Widmer, and René Levy. *Mesure et démesure du couple : cohésion, crises et résilience dans la vie des couples* (Lausanne: Payot 2008).

What I find interesting about this analytical study is that, according to the authors, even though each marital style has pluses and minuses, the **Companionship Style** is at the top of the list for happiest couples. This is precisely because we feel the most loved, respected, and supported in this configuration where we rejoice the most in our collaboration and the projects we carry out as a couple, hand in hand. What I particularly like about it is that this model couple is the only type that integrates the *big you* into the DNA of the relationship.

Worth meditating on, isn't it?

"I do not want to be the other person's EVERYTHING, and the other person is not my EVERYTHING. For me, being in a couple is being capable of combining what you have found within yourself with someone who has done the same work on awareness and self-knowledge so as not to threaten each other. I definitely do not want to be the other's everything, and I ask that the other not be my everything, either. Each of us has to already exist with ourselves and in ourselves. The basis for starting off is that I am already quite okay on my own, so I am not going to risk jeopardizing this balance, but if I can combine it with someone else, then I am even happier about it! It is already knowing how to be alone and choosing to combine that with another person. On the other hand, if the other person wants some kind of narcissistic codependence with me, I do not want that because it will cost me my freedom. So, if their pattern is to be codependent, that will send me running! I do not want to be responsible for their happiness. I am not going to take on that responsibility all on my own. I am not a savior. I do not want to go through that. It is potentially dangerous to ask that kind of thing of someone else—something they potentially cannot fulfill—because it is not their problem, and they might expect you to do the work for them. For me, my everything is the moments that I combine with the other person. And then, there is what I can do for others." [34]

Elegant, isn't it? Thank you, Theo—you summed it all up for me![35]

The Other Person Is an Event!

"Love is permanent movement. If we do not understand that love is made of impermanence, then we do not do what is necessary for it to last. Being in love is very nice, but it is temporary by nature. The principal error is having the impression that we have attained something.

In fact, that is where the movement begins! It is a constant dance. Each day, what we are and what the other person is are constant movement. Therefore, each day is a kind of constant breathing in and out that we do together so that there is harmony and success. Each day, similar to a rehearsal, there are necessary and possible aspects of innovation and creativity.

It's like cooking—you constantly have to stir the pot or it burns!" [Laughter]

"And how do you stir the pot?"

"I would be inclined to say, using some hyperbole, that the at-

---

34 Part of a conversation with Theo, a family friend, a medical student in his final year of study, and one half of a couple for quite some time.

35 Just for fun, here is a quotation from an interview with Fabrice Luchini on coupledom. "If I lived with a partner, I would expect so much for the other person to save me! If I live with a partner, the other person has to rescue me . . . . They have to make life bearable. They need to make it so that I am no longer depressed, no longer an individual. . . . I want her to kidnap me from myself, to take me out of myself! I do not want to bear anything anymore. . . . I want her to perform a miracle, for her to be miraculous. She must take me out of myself and that, that is not possible. . . . No one can take you out of yourself. I understood that no one could live for me, for that is what I expected—for someone to live my life for me."

From the television series *Vie Privée, Vie Publique* with Mireille Dumas, 2007.

Translator's Note: *Vie Privée, Vie Publique*, France 3, March 21, 2007, written by Mireille Dumas.

Fabrice Luchini is a French film and stage actor.

titude to have regarding the other person is to **view them like an event** . . . There is something that causes my perception of her to include a tiny difference in attitude, often very imperceptible . . .

"The other is like an event. I love the idea!"

"Yes, because the other person needs to be *a star!* A very intimate star, but a star that we approach with consideration . . . Because it is always a miracle to be there, together, and to feel something happening between us . . .

The other person allows us to get outside of ourselves, and, at the same time, the other person is unattainable. Love is a constant quest for the unattainable, the search for the Grail!"

A conversation with Jean-Louis Servan-Schreiber,[36] author and master of eighty springtimes, married for thirty years to Perla Servan-Schreiber. They are yin and yang; one dresses in black, the other in white.

Learn to Think of the Other Person as the Cherry on Top

Having moved away from the romantic vision of passionate, eternal love, **the little *you*** can no longer be **my exclusive purveyor** of love. It's too much to ask, as we've said. We're barking up the wrong tree. The image I have of this way of functioning is of trying to quench our thirst for love with a straw in the tiny glass of the other person when we have the whole ocean within us.

When, in fact, "if you look for it, I've got a sneaky feeling you'll find that love, actually, is all around."[37]

Hugh was right. You just have to find the right source—I have learned to see love everywhere. In words, in silences, in gestures, tears, smiles, a riff of music, a tasty dish, a ray

---

36 Translator's Note: Jean-Louis Servan-Schreiber is a French journalist. He is the founder of *Psychologies magazine* and the radio station Radio Classique, as well as the author of several books.

37 Hugh Grant in *Love Actually*, Richard Curtis's 2003 film.
Translator's Note: *Love Actually*, Netflix streaming, directed by Richard Curtis (2016; United Kingdom, United States, France: StudioCanal, Working Title Films, DNA Films, 2003).

of sunlight, a slobbery dog kiss, an embrace at the airport . . .

"All you need is love!"[38] We simply need to train ourselves to fill up our XXL supply of universal love and to share it with our cherry on top!

Learn to Love All So that You Can Love One Better

"All for one and one for all" or "all in me and me in all . . ." as a waiter in Bodh Gaya said to me. From here on out, a **big you** has become part of the little one, and it's a real big bang for me!

The **little you** is the one with whom I might potentially share a romance and want to start a life with.

The **big you** is all the others—family, friends, countrymen, humanity, you and the whole world . . .

Until recently, the *big you* never figured into my concept of romantic love. I was in a conditioned search focused on the *he-and-I-and-our-own-happiness* model of romantic love.

Today, it seems to me that the road to happiness for oneself and our alter ego is one of developing altruistic love—this jewel of veritable love. No, it is not reserved for red- or black- or white-robed monks the world over; it is available to all of us who wish to experience beautiful love stories.

This understanding first took root somewhat clearly during my encounter with the little blue butterfly in the streets of Bodh Gaya—two skinny little girls with big

---

38   "All You Need Is Love," a famous Beatles song.
      Translator's Note: The Beatles, "All You Need Is Love," by John Lennon and Paul McCartney, Parlophone, Capitol Records, 1967, MP3.

black eyes. They gave rise to an unexpected blossoming—a strange opening that grew within me day after day, connecting me to others through my heart and through actions. Thanks to my interviews with Rinpoche and to a whole slew of things, I put a **NAME** to what I was experiencing without knowing it: COMPASSION.

We have all felt this tenderness many times upon seeing someone vulnerable. We have all made many sincere acts of generosity toward people in difficulty. But perhaps we have never clearly recognized the nature of our heart's enthusiasm and given it a name: compassion. Recognizing and naming this experience allows us to give it value and meaning, to make it more concrete, and to choose to systemically repeat it. That changes everything!

Moving forward with clarity and recognition in my mind, I can train myself in full awareness and take care of my compassion like a little tree by watering it every day. This training is easy. It is no longer necessary to switch gears depending on who I'm dealing with. We're driving an automatic; we consider all beings with tenderness and that's it!

For me, compassion was the most intelligent way to relate to suffering. It allowed me to break free of the suffering of my separation, in every sense of the term. Before, I thought of myself as a little girl clinging to a life raft, lost at sea. SOS! Bit by bit, I became able to see myself as a wave among other waves in the ocean, which was a much more pleasant feeling. Today, I have this incredible feeling that I am—that we all are—the ocean. There is no more separation. Even if I know that my ego is talking 99.9 percent of the time, I get the feeling that the integration of the *big you* short circuits its neurotic patterns and connects me to this profound, basic tenderness where gentleness, strength, and joy reign.

Obviously, our capacity to love does not depend on a single person or the qualities they may or may not have. Obviously, we have infinite "opportunities to love and to experience tenderness and love. For this, we need to include the greatest number of people and beings in our hearts. For, if our kingdom contains few people, it will be a sad kingdom," as Rinpoche said to me one day.

And good news—we have over seven billion opportunities for tenderness, not counting cats, dogs, horses, cows, rabbits, guinea pigs, birds, and blue butterflies, of course!

A human being is a part of the whole, called by us "Universe," a part limited in time and space. He experiences himself, his thoughts and feelings as something separated from the rest — a kind of optical delusion of his consciousness. This delusion is a kind of prison for us, restricting us to our personal desires and to affection for a few persons nearest to us. Our task must be to free ourselves from this prison by widening our circles of compassion to embrace all living creatures and the whole of nature in its beauty.[39]

Albert Einstein

Internal Compass No. 3: #Partnership and #Caring

---

39 Excerpt from a letter by Albert Einstein written to Norman Salit, March 4, 1950. Albert Einstein Archives in Jerusalem.

And They Learn To Live Happily Ever After

#GrowingTogether

The question is, Rinpoche, "How and in what conditions did they live happily ever after?"

And they lived happily ever after is a fairytale expectation that is not based in reality. It is in the realm of the imaginary, which only has one advantage: you distract yourself for a few minutes! You cannot project this all-too-perfect desire on your partner so that he can offer it to you. This desire is also too perfect for you to offer it to him. You are not perfect, and your partner is not either. But the fairytale is! How can an imperfect person maintain a perfect role from beginning to end? It is simply impossible.

The truth is that they did not live happily ever after for the rest of their lives! They simply lived. And they learned to live happily. That is the truth. *They lived happily ever after* is a fairytale, a myth. It is an ending to stories that we should not take literally because it does not exist.

If we talk about a couple who has known each other for fifty years, we realize that they have learned to live happily together. It took them years! We could say, "Look at this couple. They have been together for fifty years. That is the best thing that could happen to a couple." Yes, but maybe it cost them a few infidelities—no, I'm kidding; that's not what I was going to say. They have loved each other, and they have hated each other. They have eaten at the same table while gazing passionately at each other. They have also wanted to kill each other or maybe secretly poison each other!

When two people are wildly in love with one another, the emotion is so strong that the opposite emotion—hatred, for example—cannot be any less strong. In fact, the person we hate the most is often the one we love the most. Some one that we do not hate at all is often some one that we could not fall in love with.

You spend time together, and you are so at ease with one another that you even know the smell of the other person's bathroom visits. I find that beautiful, and I do not understand how people do not see this beauty! There are things we do not dare to do in front of other people for fear of being judged, and yet we do them with our partners because we trust them. Of course, the other person may judge us, but there is an immense comfort within a couple, and I find that very beautiful.

The romantic idea of a couple does not begin with a real foundation, but rather based on something artificial. Look at people on dates or even in movies. There is so much pretending.

Happy relationships depend on managing our expectations. My advice is this: **expect something real, not something unreal**. Real expectations mean that you are human and that you act like human beings. Do not expect superhuman behavior. Expect something that is possible, that the other person is capable of giving. Farts are part of that; they are natural! Expect to get angry and to feel love again. These things are real. Thus, your expectations are healthy and in accordance with reality. In my opinion, *they lived happily ever after* is not true.

What is true is learning. We learn to be happy and how to make the other person happy. When we fight, we learn how to put things back together. We learn how to be patient and kind toward each other. Sometimes we are tired. That is normal—we are human! Aside from that, we try to do our best. That is what I call perfection because it is as perfect as it can be, beyond the realm of fairytales.

Our culture, books, and movies do not teach us that. They show us the exact opposite. By contrast, this book goes against the general tendency and off the beaten path. It marks a new path that allows us to discover a new landscape. In general, we act like sheep. We are happy to follow the flock. An author and a teacher should have the courage to say what they have to say, even if it is not very popular. I think we both need to be faithful to our minds. Honesty and fidelity allow us to say things in the way that we feel them, which works like a virus. I think that is what speaks to people because we are not only offering ideas, but we are communicating something real that can help them.

Three Little Things for the Road

If you had to choose three words as a conclusion on the subject of love, what would they be?
Three words—for the time that we are with the person we love? Can I say three things instead?

Okay, to sum things up . . .
When one person speaks, the other must listen. This is alarmingly simple, but often, in relationships, people wait too long to have a real conversation. When they finally have one, it is too late. Therefore, both people need to find the right moment before it is too late.

Next, it is important to **get out of the way, and let the other person express themself.** One person truly speaks, and the other person truly listens. It is not an attack-defense conversation. Each person speaks and listens in their turn, which means that there is always one person sitting back. There needs to be adaptation. We cannot both be angry at the same time, so I give the other person this time. A fight within a couple does not lead to anything good and fails horribly because both people are arguing at the same time. In the interest of the relationship, one person presents their case, while the other listens. Then, at another time, it is the opposite. The couple agrees in advance to this way of functioning; when one person presents their case, the other shuts up and listens.

And finally, it is important **never to forget the love** we feel for the other person. Remembering this during difficult moments allows you to surpass all obstacles and problems. You can scale mountains thanks to love. If you forget this love, especially repeatedly—forget mountains, you will have trouble getting up a hill. Each person needs to keep the memory of the love they feel for the other fresh in their mind.

There you go! Here are three methods that I find very efficient, if not very popular.

The first is to listen?
Yes, and when there is a fight, you let the other person present their case, and you sit and listen.

The idea is to lose?
It is not really losing. Maybe from an ordinary point of view.

And lastly, remember.
Yes. Remember love. You don't always have to lose; you just lose today.

In three words, then?
Firstly, be kind.
Next, be patient.
And lastly, love!

I know this may seem cliché, but it is the reality. The human species has overcome its many obstacles due to kindness, patience, and love. That is what scientific studies show. Whether individually or collectively, I believe we are a better society due to these qualities.

In closing, do you have any little rituals to suggest for

training ourselves to be more loving?

Sit and be!

You can begin by **meditating to calm your mind and give it stability**.

How? Sit down in a quiet place. Then, concentrate on the flow of your breathing as you inhale and exhale.

Inhale; exhale: one.
Inhale; exhale: two.
Inhale; exhale: three.

Do this until you reach twenty-one, while remaining concentrated on your breathing without forcing or putting too much pressure on yourself. On the other hand, do not be too relaxed and let your mind wander. Simply stay in the present moment with your breath. You inhale and exhale twenty-one times. If you have time, you can begin a second cycle of twenty-one breaths and a third and final cycle, as well. If you are short on time, a single cycle of twenty-one is already quite good. That takes, what, three minutes?

Three minutes a day?
Yes. The best time is before you begin your day. You develop the intention "Today, I am making an effort to do this with the goal of ___. And I want to experience___."

Can you give me an example?
I am a Buddhist master teacher, so I am not saying that the people who read what follows will practice it in exactly this way. When we begin something, the idea is not to begin with ourselves, so we set an intention. "May today be

a good day for—my dog or for so-and-so!"

This intention focuses on someone whose happiness means a lot to us.

We start our day focusing on others.

The more we act in this way, the more we open our hearts.

Our ego is in our hearts. That is why our hearts are so small! There is no space for anyone besides ourselves! Starting the day by including someone other than ourselves is a good habit. Including all sentient beings is ideal, but it is too much, so we start with the person we love the most. Then, we can add someone that we don't necessarily love, but that we don't hate either. And lastly, someone we hate. In the beginning, stick with someone you love.

By regularly practicing this, you expand your heart and leave more and more space for positive intentions for others. You can start with the person you are in love with, your parents, a friend, or why not an animal. That said, this is only the beginning. The goal is to include other people. The exercise is easy with someone we love, but it becomes less comfortable when you have to include someone you hate. That is really hard! But it is important to start at the beginning: the person you love.

At the end of the day, look at what has happened. Did the day match your intentions or not? The goal is not to ask ourselves why things worked or didn't. That would be heading off in the wrong direction. The idea is not for our day to be exactly as we wanted it to be. The essential thing is to do this exercise: to set a good intention for the day. After that, whether the day is good or not has no importance. Of course, everyone would rather have a good day and, when we do not, we immediately think, "Why did I bother to set this intention?" We only consider a relationship of cause and effect in which the cause is, "I want my day to go well, so I set that intention!" If it did go well, you would think that it works, that one plus one is two. In fact, the goal is to understand that setting the intention is an act in and of itself that creates good things. That is how I would describe this ritual.

Doing this exercise once a day—ideally at the beginning of the day—is positive. Once you have started, stick to it. Before brushing your teeth, or even while brushing your teeth, you set a positive intention. Thus, you are committing a physical act in brushing your teeth and a mental act by setting this intention. You can try to bring together these two activities as a way of developing a muscle memory. It is a synthesis of body and mind that creates a link between the two. It is a natural process, actually. The best thing is to do it when you have time—sometimes when you are brushing your teeth or sometimes when you are drinking your tea, but it should not become a dual activity. It should be its own activity. So, there is another ritual.

It is also possible to develop a bedtime ritual: a form of gratitude for what has happened during the day. If the day is good, this ritual is easy. Of course, that is often not the case! Nonetheless, we can say, "I am grateful for this day." Even if it was not good. Then, we have to ask ourselves what we are grateful for, and we will always find something to be grateful for. It is like finding a treasure in every bad experience. I promise you, there always is one! We only need the patience to discover it. We generally quit after the thought "What a bad experience. Let's not talk about it!" On the other hand, this ritual forces us to develop patience. "I want to sleep. Oh, but I have to do the ritual. Dang ritual!" Then, we have to think of something good and consider what we might be grateful for. In this way, we look at things from a different point of view, which is crucial. We do not reflect according to our usual system of thought; we have to go beyond that.

So, there are several daily rituals that you can practice. *[Silence].*

[Smiles]. Heart wide open and eyes shining with gratitude.

Hands joined at the heart. It is perfect, Rinpoche. From the depths of my heart:

THANK YOU

OFFERING!

TIBET

**Shoot for the moon. Even if you miss,
you'll land among the stars . . .**
— Oscar Wilde —

"It is organic!" Rinpoche said it from the very beginning.

Ever since I was ten years old—after reading a book[40] that spirited me away, I dreamed of visiting the roof of the world. Today, after nine months in the abyss, I am at the top of a mountain pass—sixteen thousand feet of altitude, hair blown by the wind, arms thrown out in a great V. It is a sign of victory. I did it! Realizing my dream is a strange feeling. It is like going to a very important meeting or finding a source of inner strength, enthusiasm, inspiration . . .

I LIVE AGAIN!

I have travelled so many roads in the last nine months, from Normandy to Bodh Gaya to Paris to Toronto, and,

---

40   Rampa, T. Lobsang. *The Third Eye: The Autobiography of a Tibetan Lama*. London, Secker and Warburg, 1950.

finally, to the majestic mountains of Tibet! Looking out at the immensity of the sky, the wild, natural beauty of the landscape, the turquoise sacred lakes, and the colored prayer flags fluttering in the wind, my heart swells like a hot air balloon. Right here and now, in this moment, I wish I could fly out to the four corners of the Earth to share with you the joy that sparkles in my mind.

#Offering!

Thank you to the *kindness of the situation*, which has been a true light in the dark! They say we experience this most in difficult situations—surely because they carry within them a potential for kindness that illuminates who we are to ourselves. When we get shaken up, we can say, "Look, an opportunity to become aware of what is happening within me!"

Lately, I have had a lot of opportunities. Though it was a serious demolition of my ego, the breakup offered me the opportunity to discover myself, my personal film, and my individual projections of romantic love—nothing is black and white.

When the Lumière brothers gave one of the first public projections in the history of film more than one hundred and twenty years ago—*Arrival of a Train at a Station*—they say that people were frightened. Spectators thought that the locomotive was going to charge right into them, and they ran for the back of the theater. If someone had told me before that altruistic love and compassion would become part of my idea of romantic love, I would have fled as well.

And yet, when passion broke my heart, it is indeed compassion that brought me back. It really was the most intelligent way to connect with my suffering and become free from it. I am thankful every day.

Faithful to the Tibetan tradition of hanging prayer flags on mountaintops and passes and trail crossings, I offered flags of blue-white-red-green-yellow, printed with sacred words, to the winds. Then, hands joined at my heart, I made wishes of love and happiness for all of you and for you, reading this book . . .

Then, I made wishes of love and happiness for all of you.

May all sentient beings have happiness and the causes of happiness!
May all sentient beings be free from suffering and the causes of suffering!
May all sentient beings never be parted from happiness free from suffering!
May all sentient beings abide in equanimity, free from bias, attachment,
and aversion![41]

Remember, the equation is simple:
Closed Heart = Fear and Solitude
Open Heart = Love and Serenity

Good news! The sun is here, within us, and always has been . . .

To you, and you, and you, and you, and you too . . . and to all of you, I wanted to say . . .

I love you!

#AllYouNeedIsLove
May you ALL experience the causes for happiness!

---

41   Wishing prayer of the four limitless thoughts.

Acknowledgements

Thank you to all. You fill my heart.

Thank you to the Three Jewels.

Thank you to the Venerable, 5th Dilyag Sabchu Rinpoche, my spiritual friend, who, in a certain way, brought me back to life. #Armageddon

Thank you to Mipham Chökyi Lodrö, the 14th Shamar Rinpoche and Thaye Dorje, the 17th Karmapa.

Thank you to my children, Alexis and Anastasia Regen.

Thank you to my friends and loves: Liz Van Gelder, Christophe Fauré, Pascale Guerin, Soizic Michelot, Monica Degli Esposti, Barbara Martin, Charline Redin, Annaik Dokhan, Pascal Regen and Ursula Saint Leger, Charlotte de Fouchier, Anael Assier, Fabien Berger, Ivan Goldstein, Joseph Macé Scaron, Maxime Rovere, Lionel Choukroun, Gonzague De Larocque, Céline, Sébastien, Nathalie, Natacha Calestreme, Sébastien Delaby, Julia Stentzel, Sidney Bone, Nicolas Jammet, Lama Puntso.

An eternal thank you to Marc Levy.

A special thank you to Jean-Louis Servan Schreiber.

Thank you, from the depths of my heart, to all those whom I love, all those who support me and accompany me, all those who have helped me with this book, from near or far, and all those with whom I have had the pleasure of talking, laughing, dancing, and crying.

Thank you to Arnaud Duhayon, Audrey Desserrières, Nicolas Jammet, Anael Assier, Gilles Seigneurgens.

Thank you to the little blue butterfly.

Thank you to A for *Amour*, who allowed me to discover another, much vaster love.

Thank you to all these masters and servants of beauty who nourish my heart. In no particular order: Terrence Malick, Wong Kar-wai, Mark Rothko, Vincent van Gogh, Francis Bacon, Jean-Michel Basquiat, Giacometti, Bram van Velde, Rilke, Baudelaire, Marguerite Duras, Annie Lennox, Vivaldi, Bach, Mozart, Sting, Schopenhauer, Spinoza, Nietzche, Lou Andreas Salomé, Marina Abramovic, Sylvie Guillem, JR, Mikhail Baryshnikov, Benjamin Pech, Prince, U2, Massive Attack, Archive—and all the others!

Thank you to all the *you* I have encountered, met, loved or hated, and with whom I have shared, travelled, exchanged, learned—who have made me, surprised me, inspired me, and allowed me to "fly high and contemplate the vastness," and,

Don't forget—you are all buddhas!

Acknowledgements from Sabchu Rinpoche:

Thank you to Mipham Chökyi Lodrö, the 14th Shamar Rinpoche.

Printed in June 2019
by Pulsio
Publisher Number : 4004
Legal Deposit : July 2019
Printed in Bulgaria